SPARK

A Blueprint to Reignite Purpose

ERICKA ELLIS

ISBN:

Editor: Sharp Editorial, LLC

Dedication

Ty and Tyler, you make me better. I love you deeply.

Table of Contents

Acknowledgments vii

A Message From the Author xi

Introduction: Trial by Fire xvii

Chapter One: Stay Connected 1

Chapter Two: Perspective Is Key 27

Chapter Three: Address Your Fears 41

Chapter Four: Respect the Process 67

Chapter Five: Know Who You Are 93

Final Thoughts 119

About the Author: Ericka Ellis 123

Acknowledgments

I am so thankful for those who were intimately involved with this project. Your commitment through this process demonstrates more than support. It demonstrates your love. Your creativity, research, resources, time, and wisdom have been invaluable gifts to me. I cannot thank you enough.

Taryn, you were such a delightful, patient, and encouraging friend and graphic designer who worked diligently to deliver the vision I could not articulate at times. Thank you for your expertise, time, and creativity. Your excitement throughout this process helped light an amazing fire under me. I am forever grateful to you.

DeAndre, thank you for challenging me to dig deeper so I could articulate my experiences and revelations to make a greater impact. This book would not be half as effective or enjoyable (lol) if I did not have your insight and input. Thank you for sacrificing so much of your time, from the inception to completion of this book. I could not have done it without you.

To my editor, Laci Swann. Your promptness, attention to detail, and professionalism were critical to this project. Thank you for being diligent, responsive, and honest with your feedback.

To my incredibly supportive husband, Ty. My success is a reflection of your sacrifice and selflessness. As you continue to accomplish your dreams, you remind me that I can do anything. Because of you, I really believe I can do it all: be a great wife to you, mother to our children, and a vessel for the Lord. Thank you for encouraging me to see myself the way God sees me. I am better because of you.

To my son, Tyler. Thank you for reminding Mommy of who I am. Your divine wisdom at such timely moments was exactly what I needed to show up for my destiny. "Mommy, you are the Fire Starter! You inspire people! Finish your book!" I will never forget how often God used your tiny voice to speak major confirmations and revelations into my life. I love you so much.

To all my friends who have encouraged me, believed in me, and supported me in everything I do, *thank you!* I could not go on this journey without any of you.

"But a tiny spark can set a great forest on fire."

(JAMES 3:5)

A Message From the Author

"Fan into the flames."

(2 Timothy 1:6)

Before my SPARK experience, I overloaded on self-help books, personal development podcasts, newsletters, and articles – most without biblical backing – to overcome the disconnect I had with my purpose. None of those resources worked because I was trying to apply secular answers to spiritual problems. I knew I was called by God, but I did not understand why voices of fear, apathy, and identity crisis were constantly calling out for me, too. As much as I tried to ignore those diversions with my self-help solutions, my performance and productivity never changed. It was not until God revealed that the weight of my purpose could never be supported by the words of the world. I needed *His* answers. I needed to seek *His* face. When I started exploring His Word more than the World Wide Web, life started to change. *God* set me on fire! "Self" could never set a soul on fire who has been called by God. I had to get away from the world's idea of purpose, stop relying on those strategies, and partner with God to see real progress in my life.

But it all started with a spark.

God took me on a transformative journey to uncover hidden fears, a broken identity, and my misguided faith. That is how this book was birthed – through real pain, frustrations, and setbacks. Every chapter is a result of life experiences and revelations that provided the wisdom I needed to move forward in purpose. Through my SPARK experience, I had to learn *real* productivity in the eyes of the Lord, and what I learned was that God created us to be *fruitful,* not productive.

Productivity is *doing* the work.

Fruitfulness is a *result* of the work.

I was so busy trying to learn how to be productive by setting S.M.A.R.T. goals, using time-management resource tools, and setting deadlines, yet I never managed to see real fruit. That is because fruit does not come from doing the work. It comes from God doing the work within you. That is why you are struggling with your purpose – because you thought you could do it on your own. The success of your productivity is based on whether you allow God to do the work within you. *That* is the game-changer.

SPARK is an acronym divided into chapter units that are designed to be your blueprint for success. This guide uniquely exposes the root of your unproductivity while simultaneously providing practical solutions to your problem. This blueprint is essential for reigniting your purpose, so you can accomplish what God has called you to do. SPARK is not just an acronym to achieve success. SPARK is the answer to your burnout. When you lose your fire of courage, faith, and consistency, that is an indicator you need to refuel through the strategies provided in SPARK.

Allow the SPARK method to act as a divine guide to help you break past the pitfalls that interfere with being fruitful and on fire.

I know you have dreams, goals, and visions that make your heart flutter, maybe even bring tears to your eyes, but this is when you must decide not just to hear the Word but *do* what the Word says. Do not let SPARK act as just another self-help book like the books of my past. This is *your* blueprint. This is your how, why, and what. Do not waste another day on fear, perfectionism, self-doubt, laziness, and any other spiritual barrier that may be holding you back. You must decide that you will not go through another calendar year of unchecked boxes and incomplete tasks. Those empty boxes are more than a physical sign of your unproductivity; they are symbolic of the emptiness in your spirit. Being unproductive and unfruitful will always breed unfulfillment.

If these sentiments sound familiar, do not let tomorrow be a repeat of yesterday or today. Friend, a life half lived is not a full life. That is not the life God wants any of us to live. You were created to be fruitful and multiply. Stop dividing your focus and subtracting from your faith. You could never multiply the gifts and talents God has given you when you function through a broken formula.

Here is the truth about having dreams associated with your purpose. Dreams give us an adrenaline rush... but to where? We rush off in a hurry to dream, but this rush rarely pushes us to *complete* our dreams. Dreaming is only a stimulant. Completion is where we find true satisfaction. If you struggle with completing what you started and fail to see fruit in your life, do not be discouraged. God's grace is infinite and will cover the days you feel you have lost. However, the time has come to do better. In fact, the time has come to do *more*. It is time to produce more *fruit* in your life. When you produce, you honor your true self, and, most importantly, you honor the Lord.

If fear is the culprit for your lack of zeal, I want to encourage you to have *appropriate fear*. That is, fear of the Lord –

Fear of disappointing Him.

Fear of wasting valuable gifts and talents.

Fear of living a life below your potential.

Fear of being in the same place next year.

Fear of dealing with the same insecurities and jealousies.

Fear of living a life of regret.

Those fears can be appreciated because they produce *change*, but do not allow yourself to become comfortable with those feelings. Instead, allow those fears to act as motivation.

If you have been going through the motions, decide today that you will live with a sense of urgency. Decide today that you will be fruitful! Only you and God know what that looks like. Repent for the days you have wasted and rejoice for the time you have to get it done. And remember, to keep your momentum, you must do it by *faith* because nothing accelerates momentum more than faith. Faith is your fuel, your oxygen, and your fire!

I believe in you, and it is time to start believing in yourself.

As you continue your journey, refer to SPARK as often as needed. This book is not to be viewed as a page-turner but a page finder. Utilize SPARK as the blueprint it was created for – your resource to guide you through your journey of purpose. No more stopping, making excuses, or waddling in discouragement. Just as God equipped me with spiritual strategies to respond to the call over my life, SPARK will provide support and strategies for you, too. SPARK is your leaping pad to jumpstart you into action *and* completion to become the trailblazer you desire to be. It is time to fan into the flames of the spiritual gift God put inside of you! The fire will come, but it starts with a SPARK. The time has come to do the work and let God do His work within you.

With love,

Ericka Ellis

Introduction

Trial by Fire

Do you want to know why I wrote this book?

I wrote this book because I was a hot mess, struggling with constant burnouts in pursuit of my purpose. I knew, deep in my soul, there was at least one other person who felt the same and wanted to know why.

Why am I unproductive?

Why can't I push past these feelings?

Is something wrong with me?

Am I lazy?

Why is this so difficult?

Why can't I stay motivated?

Am I truly gifted?

Am I good enough?

Is this what I am supposed to be doing?

Those taunting thoughts were destroying me. I would lose my momentum and my fire, leaving me unfulfilled and discouraged. You see, when you lose your fire, you lose your confidence and begin to question everything, from who you are to what you are meant to do. Worse, you begin to question if God chose the right person for the task. Those questions lead to a mental interrogation that has the potential to destroy dreams, hopes, and purpose, and if you allow it, your destiny will turn into ashes from the wildfire of doubt.

If you are anything like the former me, birthing ideas is not the problem. The inspiration to act on those ideas is the issue at hand. Formerly, bright idea after bright idea would come flooding in my mind, but each idea was always left on the shore, piling up like a collection of seashells. Like you, I searched for answers, only to realize I was looking in the wrong places. Secular self-help books no longer served the deep calling over my life. I did not need to hear another motivational speech or sermon about purpose, and I did not need to be convinced about my gifts and talents. Truth be told, I already believed I was gifted, and I hope you know you are gifted, too. The problem was, I did not know *why* I was not putting my gifts to good use on a consistent basis. There was a fire burning deep in my soul, waiting for me to pursue greatness. At the same time, my mind was a water hose, extinguishing those flames. I was a walking contradiction. I was the "Fire Starter" with no fire. Go figure.

Some days, I would be on fire, relentlessly pursuing my purpose. Other days, my flame would barely flicker because of fear, doubt, or toxic habits I had yet to break. Somehow, I slipped into autopilot, physically, mentally, and spiritually. Worse, I tried to keep up with the images of purpose through outlets of Instagram and Facebook, which, unfortunately, have become the standard for proving success or a life well-lived. When used for self-serving reasons, social media is a dangerous, superficial trap to an authentic, God-given purpose, and I felt myself falling into that toxicity. Commonly, people share their accomplishments via social media, tied to the phrase "Won't He do it?!" but the rest of the caption screams, "I'm the one who really did it!" We give Him a shout-out while putting the spotlight on us. That cannot be purpose, and that is certainly not an expression of genuine gratitude. Reading those types of statuses and captions make me squirm because of the obsession with ego, and my spirit grieves when I recall those very images I used to seek recognition and validation from strangers.

Through online engagement, purpose started to look like another self-promoting gimmick, and living up to the hype was easy – smile for the camera, write an inspiring quote, and share a contrived picture and manufactured words with the world. One can easily skip every step required for purpose when distracted by the *image* of purpose. Eventually, painting the perfect picture grows old, as that mode of living is always unfulfilling. My spirit was tired of the superficial, and my artificial expression of purpose was not moving me closer to God's destiny for my life.

Trying to keep up with one image after another led me nowhere. Literally, nowhere. I was stuck in the same place, distracted by an image – the appearance of having life all together.

I was unfulfilled.

I was confused.

I was frustrated.

I second-guessed my calling.

I justified my inactivity to waiting to hear from God.

Days turned to weeks, and weeks turned to months. You know how it goes – your blazing, bright idea flickers until your dream goes up in smoke.

That is where I was for over a year – waiting, justifying, and stuck.

Don't get me wrong – during that time, I would jump in and out of the picture with some form of evidence of behind the scenes "hard work," but at the end of the day, I was living with the proofs of still images of idleness. Day to day, I would pray, "God, show me what to do next," but my eyes were not really on Him. I would glance up because that is the polite thing to do when making a prayer request, but once the request was over, so was the steadiness of my heart and spirit. I would wander around for the rest of the day, justifying sitting on my hands rather than working with them.

The truth is, there are many reasons why people stop in their tracks on the journey of purpose – fear, insecurities, and complacency, to name a few – and I will dive into those disruptions, plus more, in this book. I know all about those distractions and pitfalls because I have experienced them, often experiencing multiple distractions in one day.

The purpose of this book is to help you experience less burnout and more fire. I will help you identify the fire extinguishers in your life by taking you through my journey, consequently exposing the root of idleness, identity crisis, fear, and the negative emotions that held me back from blazing my fiery trail, which, perhaps, are the very reasons for the current burnout in your life.

This book will transform your spiritual walk and how you pursue purpose. What many do not understand is that *purpose is a journey of becoming.* Purpose is a process of transformation that leads you to a passion while igniting a stronger love between you and the Lord. *Purpose has a purpose,* and its priority is always on the person first, not the goal. The journey of purpose is a refining process that will always produce something *in* you before it can produce something *from* you.

You will learn how to push past these mental barriers and regain your momentum with an unstoppable fire! You will regain clarity, courage, connectivity, and the consistency to keep you fueled to live your life at an optimal level. By the end of this book, you will be the trailblazer God predestined you to be. The time has come to revive you back to your purpose and the God who gave it to you. Are you ready to get your SPARK back? Now is the time to ignite your fire *and* keep it!

Chapter One

Stay Connected

Introduction: This Part

This book is written in several parts to help you identify and prevent some of the primary issues interfering with your momentum in pursuing your purpose. Every chapter is significant; however, Chapter One matters *the most*. You can do everything in this book, but if you skip *this part*, you are skipping over the fire. You may see some progress, but you will never have the enthusiasm or momentum you really want and need if you close this book at Chapter One. This is the part that separates the ordinary from the extraordinary. I must admit, this is the hard part, and, honestly, spiritual discipline was *the* most difficult part for me. There have been many days I compromised staying connected to God because I was ready to jump into my day. But it never failed; when I missed this part, I was immediately overwhelmed, I lacked productivity, and an entire day of opportunity had been wasted. I had to learn it would be impossible to stay connected to my purpose without staying connected to the One who gave it to me.

Staying connected is hard because this part requires more of you. In fact, this part requires *all of you*. Staying connected requires daily intentional sacrifice and commitment that you may have never exercised to this extent in your life. But this is why I am warning you now – this spiritual discipline is not going to be easy but staying connected will always produce your fire. If you are serious about regaining your fire, you must get serious about *this part*. You cannot neglect this part because this is the part that requires your *spirit*. Your fire cannot survive without allowing God to set your spirit ablaze. This is how you become a trailblazer – God sets your spirit ablaze and lights up the path before you as you pursue your goals. You cannot be a trailblazer without being in partnership with God. He lights up the trail *and* you!

Fire comes at a cost, and if you are willing to pay the price of sacrifice, surrender, and submission, then you will realize *this part* is an *invitation* to experience God's presence that will produce more than a fire in your life, but a *promise*. This part gives access to the supernatural fire that will allow you to produce and perform at your best. Once you have that fire, the following chapters will add to your burning flame, creating an unstoppable fire in your life. This book will provide you with the spark that has been missing yet has always been available. It is time to let that flame rise, but remember, it can only happen if you do *this part*.

The Vine and the Branches

My phone has many capabilities, but my phone is useless if it has not been properly charged. The smartphone performs some of the most innovative tasks at our fingertips, but it cannot fully function at its optimal potential if it does not have sufficient energy. The phone carries out the features assigned to it, but the charger gives the phone its *power*.

The phone can only perform to the extent of the power provided by the charger. Without the charger, the phone would not have any power; it would be useless. The same notion applies to you. *Your gifts and purpose are useless if you do not stay connected to God's power.*

How often do you become distracted by the ideas and gifts God has given you that you miss the opportunity to connect with Him? Perhaps your rise and fall go a little something like this...

You see your potential and feel incredibly excited. You create vision boards, strategies, outlines, and plans that look like a shoo-in to success, but in a matter of time, something happens. Your creativity starts to flicker, your confidence goes up in smoke, and you begin running on fumes because of the shortage of power. You officially reached burnout. You have lost your focus, discipline, confidence, and enthusiasm to work on your goals.

Why?

The answer is simple: the energy you started with could not last long enough to see you through your journey of purpose. Willpower could never be enough. Only God's power can sustain you. Like your smartphone, you must recharge your battery daily. You lose momentum because you do not have any power, like a car that runs out of gas. Eventually, that car will stop. If you want completion, you must stay connected.

I know that staying connected is difficult, but nothing is as difficult as waking up every day, feeling drained, unmotivated, unfulfilled, and uninspired to live your best life.

To have the energy and motivation to pursue your goals, you must stay connected. In fact, Jesus said it, plain and simple: "*I am the true vine.*

You are the branches. Stay joined to me, and I will stay joined to you. No branch can produce fruit alone. It must stay connected to the vine. It is the same with you. You cannot produce fruit alone. You must stay joined to me" (John 15:1-5).

These scriptures helped me understand what "staying connected" truly signified. Before this understanding, I minimized this concept to activity – you know, the daily routine of a five-minute devotional and a quick prayer, and then it's on with your day? But God showed me I had this concept all wrong. Staying connected was not a matter of being active but an opportunity for *activation*. The routine is a prerequisite to connect with God *but not the focus.* Your focus should be on the activation – God activating His supernatural power of confidence, clarity, and enthusiasm into you for the day. That focused energy is the reward for staying connected. The experience depends on your *focus.* Are you focused on the routine or the reward? Never choose the mindless activity of going through the motions over being set ablaze through an *intentional* experience. Every connection is an opportunity to access God's power to perform and produce beyond your ability.

Jesus said: *"Remain in me, and I will remain in you. For a branch cannot produce fruit if it is severed from the vine, and you cannot be fruitful unless you remain in me"* (John 15:4).

The confidence you need?

The clarity and direction you desire?

The proper mindset?

Those feats come only by way of the connection. God activates those characteristics in your life when you connect to His power. You will produce better and greater from His presence. Friend, you are to be like the branches in the following verse: *"I am the true vine. You are the branches. Stay joined to me and I will stay joined to you. No branch can produce fruit alone. It must stay connected to the vine"* (John 15:1-3).

Notice the scripture stated that the branch does not have to do anything but stay, abide, and remain. The branch benefits from the life of the vine simply because it is connected. There is nothing else you need to do other than stay connected! When you are connected, you naturally produce the ideas God had in mind for you, *organically.* There is no forcing, only flowing.

Here is the truth: You cannot create anything. You can only *bear* what God gives you. He creates it, and He lets you bear it. Do you know what bear means? Bear means to be responsible for, to hold, and to carry. You cannot produce purpose. You are only responsible for *carrying* out the purpose God has given you. So, that vision you have? You did not magically come up with that. God was generous enough to gift that to you. *"For it is God who works in you to will and to act in order to fulfill his good purpose"* (Philippians 2:13). Your desire to accomplish your goal is noble, but your desire is not enough. You can only accomplish your goals by delighting yourself in His presence. Psalm 37:4 confirms this: *"Take delight in the Lord, and he will give you your heart's desires."*

However, when you are disconnected from God, you bear the burdens of your disappointments, doubts, and discouragement. You incessantly grind your gears, only to set you back in time and resources. Consequently, you remain stuck and feel burned out. Most times, burnout is a result of relying more on your ability than His anointing.

For years, that was my life in a nutshell. I would get my quick charge from God, and days later, I wondered why I felt unqualified, confused, and on the verge of giving up and choosing another "purpose." I had to learn to resist the temptation to live a life separate from Jesus. Have you ever wondered why you wander as often as you do, knowing you love and need God? I can tell you why – disconnecting is easy. It is easier to live a life without intention and self-discipline, but you will quickly learn, as I did, that the consequences weigh heavily on you like a ton of bricks. Digging myself out of that pit stole the energy and time I could have put toward my goals and relationship with God. Take it from me – you must learn to resist the easy road that does not include God. The easy road is a lonely path that produces *nothing*. In other words, you need Jesus for everything. That's right, every single thing.

Jesus declares, *"Yes, I am the vine; you are the branches. Those who remain in me, and I in them, will produce much fruit. For apart from me you can do nothing"* (John 15:5).

He said that without Him, you can do nothing! Nothing excludes *nothing…* at least nothing of significance – that includes being confident, disciplined, strategic, proactive, and faithful, all the pieces you need on this journey of purpose. You could never be as productive or fruitful apart from God.

Staying connected creates visions.

Staying connected makes up for lost time.

Staying connected opens doors.

Staying connected accelerates the process.

Staying connected is the beginning of completion.

Staying connected allows you to function *beyond* your natural capabilities.

If you want more power, you must stay connected!

The Power of Sacrifice

You may be thinking, "Okay, Ericka, I get it – 'Stay connected,' but how? What does staying connected even look like?"

Staying connected starts with sacrifice.

There are many ways to define sacrifice, but here is my definition: Sacrifice is giving up one thing for something *better.*

When you look at sacrifice from that point of view, it seems there is no loss but only a win, right? However, many people view sacrifice negatively.

Think about it.

When you give up your favorite foods because you started a new workout plan, you become so focused on what you are giving up rather than the reward of what is to come. The transformation is the promise you should focus on, but the sacrifice steals your attention and is perceived as a punishment. The sacrifice no longer seems worth the result because of the cost. However, the focus should always be on the future benefit, not the present loss. Nevertheless, sacrifice is where many people become stuck. If you want an unstoppable fire in your life, you must understand the importance of sacrifice.

The type of sacrifice I am referring to is *total submission* – submitting your mind, body, spirit, and will to God so that He can do something greater in you. When you fail to submit, you are ultimately rejecting the fire. You must understand and accept this concept – *God is the fire, you are the sacrifice,* and *then* you are set ablaze by Him.

God's Word put sacrifice in perspective for me. In Leviticus 9:24, the scripture shares how God started a fire on the altar *after* there was a sacri-

7

fice. This demonstrates how important it is for God to see what you are willing to offer Him in exchange for His power. This scripture goes on to say, *"Fire blazed forth from the Lord's presence and consumed the burnt offering and fat on the altar."* The fire came out of God's presence! This was when I realized we could not create that fire. I tried, for so long, to manufacture a fire that would not give. No wonder I could not shake the fear, doubt, and apathy in my life! I would skip past staying connected to God because I did not like the idea of sacrificing my pride, routine, and excuses. The penalty of rejecting sacrifice will always lead to self-sabotage. Skipping over this step is a setback. Therefore, daily submission to God is vital. If you are not connected, you cannot catch fire. The fire comes only when you have something to give God to set ablaze.

Just as the scripture above illustrated the fire coming from God *after* the sacrifice on the altar, the same goes for you. God sets the heart on fire that has already offered a sacrifice. Maybe you are wondering, "How can I be a sacrifice?" It is quite simple: Give yourself to Him.

The Bible better explains it in Romans 12:1: *"I plead with you to give your bodies to God because of all He has done for you. Let them be a living and holy sacrifice—the kind He will find acceptable. This is truly the way to worship Him."*

To be a living sacrifice means surrendering every part of you to God as an act of worship, from your heart to your head to your feet. Surrendering is saying to God, "Here is my mind, transform it. God, let the words of my mouth and the meditation of my heart be pleasing to You. Help my eyes stay focused on You and see the good in what You are doing and the people around me. Let my hands do the work You want them to do.

Keep me from being idle. Keep my feet from treading in the wrong direction. Keep me from deliberate sin."

This is how you are a living sacrifice: *You give God all you have because you know He will give you all you need.* Friend, *you* are the sacrifice. Your heart is the sacrifice. Your willingness to submit under God's authority is the sacrifice. This is the start of your activation. You are ready to be set on fire, but how do you keep the fire going?

How to Sustain the Fire

Sacrifice is one part of staying connected to God. You might be wondering, "So, after I lay it all out, what's next?" Let's go back to the scripture that revolutionized (for me) what an intentional relationship with God looks like. The scripture tells us that *after* God consumed the altar with His fire, He gave strict instructions to the priests to care of the fire. He told the people: *"Remember, the fire must be kept burning on the altar at all times. It must never go out. Each morning the priest will add fresh wood to the fire… Remember, the fire must be kept burning on the altar at all times. It must never go out"* (Leviticus 6:12-13).

When I first read that scripture, it blew my mind! I had cried and complained so much, asking and wondering why my fire would burn out in just a matter of days, not realizing I was the problem. I assumed since I *needed* consistent power, God was supposed to give it to me, but I would eventually discover that keeping the fire was *my* job.

I have learned there is always an action attached to our request.

This scripture proves that *you* have a responsibility to keep the fire burning. God lights your fire, but you maintain the fire. Staying connected is a daily practice that God left you accountable to do. Just as God told the priests in the scripture, you are to care for the fire "every morning," "add fresh wood daily," and it "must be kept burning," you are charged with the same instructions.

What does this look like in a practical sense?

Simply put, it is creating time to connect with God daily.

Yes, every day.

I have tried, time and time again, to get around this but soon learned that avoiding daily worship is the quickest and surest way to lose my fire, the fire of persistence, productivity, and peace and the will to push through. If, for some reason, your day does not start until the afternoon or evenings due to your job, school, and so forth, this notion still applies but is unique to the start of *your* day.

You must bring fresh wood of sacrifice by way of prayer, praise, or worship, first thing in the morning, just as the scripture illustrates. This daily spiritual practice means *first thing*. If you delay connecting with God, you will have allowed the world to get to you before allowing God to touch you. Normal day-to-day activities, such as morning traffic, your quirky co-worker, or getting your children ready for the day, have a greater chance of negatively impacting your attitude, which could potentially affect your performance and productivity. That is because you have missed a chance to sit in God's presence to receive the grace and strength needed for that day.

Think of yourself as an empty cup. Without first connecting with God, life's circumstances fill your cup. The frustrations, incidentals, stressful interactions, and so forth sit within you, affecting your attitude and behavior. However, if you connect with God first, He acts as a solvent that has already been poured into you, protecting you from being contaminated with the cares of the world. Scientifically speaking, a solvent creates solutions. God is your solution. He has already solved whatever problem you may encounter because He has poured into you first. As a supernatural Solvent, God neutralizes your thinking to be proactive rather than reactive. In other words, you will most likely have the mind of God to respond appropriately to whatever circumstance that may present itself because you prioritized sitting in His presence. God knows this, as you only have a limited strength on your own. If you connect with Him *first*, you will be more effective and empowered to deal with situations more productively. Spending time with God, first thing, changes the entire trajectory of the day for your good. God is divine in that way; you give Him a fraction, and He will give you more.

The Bible reminds you to *"Seek first the Kingdom of God above all else, and live righteously, and he will give you everything you need"* (Matthew 6:33). Based on that scripture, you should notice how prioritizing God will *automatically* position you to get everything you need. You may think you are losing time by sitting still, but God has a supernatural way of multiplying time in your favor. Change the way you think about your connection, and you will experience an abundance of clarity and energy and increased performance. The Bible tells us that anything you try to accomplish for the Lord cannot be done in your own might or power but by His Spirit (Zechariah 4:6). Sitting in God's presence is the key to your productivity.

Staying connected is not to be confused with activity. Staying connected is an opportunity to remain in God's presence, to grow, and to accomplish the goals He placed in your heart. Every time you actively engage your faith by connecting with God, you are sustaining your fire, and, more importantly, you are sustaining your relationship with the Lord. God desires a *close* relationship with you, but it is up to you to keep that spark alive.

But how?

How do you stay connected?

The following sections will give you a clear understanding of how to develop a long-lasting connection to God while keeping you ablaze.

Intimacy

Intimacy is *the* key to sustaining your fire because to catch fire, you must be close to it. Since God is the fire, intimacy is the fuel to keep you ablaze. Though the solution may seem simple, practicing intimacy is challenging for most people. The challenge is accepting the fact that intimacy requires *unceasing engagement*. You must be deeply committed to putting forth this type of required effort. As I mentioned earlier, this is the part most people run from because staying connected through intimacy is challenging. The required attention to detail, responsiveness, and devotion may seem a bit demanding, but this is a commitment that is developing an impenetrable connection. Intimacy is often confused with a relationship-centered around sex, but the truth is, intimacy is a relationship rooted in *connection*. If you are committed to staying connected to God, and I believe you are, then you must be committed to cultivating intimacy with Him.

Intimacy is illustrated through communication, respect, and quality time. Those are the cornerstones of a healthy connection in any relationship, especially a connection with the Lord. You may be wondering how those qualities of intimacy relate to connecting with God. This spiritual connection looks like *spending time* with Him in His **Word**, *communicating* with Him through **prayer,** and *respecting* Him through **worship**. Those are the fundamental qualities that will sustain your fire and relationship with the Lord. It is that simple.

Unfortunately, many of us get stuck in developing intimacy because we do not know what that looks like in a practical sense, or we are held back by pride, a lack of trust, or past mistakes. The following pages will better equip you with the tools you need to identify the causes of your disconnection and the practical ways to overcome those hurdles.

Quality Time

To keep this concept applicable, think about your current relationships. Whether family, co-workers, or a companion, before you knew them, you had to *get to know* them by *spending time* with them. Getting to know someone is a gradual process that eventually evolves into a secure and trusted relationship. This is also true for your connection with God. Spending time with God means spending time in His Word and getting to know His character as a deity and as your Father. You learn to trust God through His Word because you discover who He is and how He cares for you. Reading the Bible allows you to journey into the depths of God's character, discovering an unconditional and faithful love that He has for you. In time, you begin to accept that God is deeply committed to you, no matter your sin or circumstances, but you will never learn to have a secure, trusted relationship with God if you do not get to know Him.

If you struggle with knowing what to read or "how" to read the Bible, my suggestion is to start with the Gospels. The Gospels are a great way to familiarize yourself with the heart of the Lord to strengthen your faith and relationship with Him. The Gospels illustrate God's love through His Son, Jesus, which reveals His character and affections toward you. The Gospels demonstrate God's mercy, grace, compassion, and sacrificial love for you.

It would also be beneficial for you to read the Book of Proverbs to add to your growing knowledge of the Lord and His expectations of you. Proverbs is God's way of giving you spiritual insight and instructions for your everyday life. The Book of Proverbs personifies His expectations for how you should carry yourself to live a moral, peaceful, and successful life. If you want to know what God, your Father, expects of you, His child, read the Book of Proverbs. Not only will you get to know Him, but you will learn what He expects of you, too.

Lastly, if you simply want to learn how to study the Bible in a new way, I suggest using a concordance (many are in the back of your Bible). A concordance acts as a biblical GPS, helping you navigate relevant subjects in alphabetical order and directing you to the appropriate scripture(s) on the topic you want to study.

There are many ways to dive into the pages of God's Word, so do not ever think there is a wrong way to do it. The art of reading God's Word is a matter of reading it with an open mind and an open heart. Opening the pages at random could be beneficial to you because God's Word is living and active. What you may perceive as coincidental is God's divine way of being intentional. No matter how you decide to journey through the pages of God's divinity, you will learn who He is and who He is to you.

Through this transparent experience, you establish a secure relationship with God because you learn He can, indeed, be trusted. Because of this trust, you will begin to take on the identity of His nature that will positively affect the relationship you have with Him. Acquiring this kind of understanding of God can only happen when you spend quality time with Him. I dare you to open your Bible, dig deep into the pages, and discover the mysteries of God that He only reveals when you make time to get to know Him. If you want to spend quality time with Him, you must do it in the way He left for us – through His Word.

Communication

In addition to spending time with God in His Word, you must always find time to communicate with Him. Constant communication with God is where you get your power! This level of intimacy is comparable to the chemistry you experience in your relationships. It is a sensation that makes you feel more connected to a person's energy and spirit. The same is true with prayer.

Since spending time in His Word reveals who He is, opening in prayer *should* be an easy task for you because you know *Who* you are talking to. However, prayer does not come easy for most people. From experience, I have found the disconnect of prayer to be rooted in several things – minimizing this experience to just "talking," a lack of desire to pray, and not knowing what to share. Worse, there is the fear of being vulnerable with God. Vulnerability is the foundation of prayer, but if you struggle with being vulnerable, you will pull away in pride and shame because you do not want God to see the *real* you, the real you who is broken, flawed, sinful, unforgiving, and so forth. You must understand that your pride is robbing you of experiencing the power of prayer the way it was designed.

Prayer was designed to bring healing, hope, and confidence in your life, but many people do not experience this because they do not approach prayer with *humility*. God distinctly says: *"If my people, which are called by my name, shall humble themselves, pray and seek my face and turn from their wicked ways, then I will hear from heaven…"* (2 Chronicles 7:14).

God hears you when you *humbly* come to Him. He is not surprised by your hang-ups. He knows you well, but when you openly share the truth about who you are and where you are in life, your guards fall, and *God has a way in.*

That is how you experience the power of prayer!

You have given God the right to enter your heart to comfort you, transform you, and heal you. If you want to experience the power of prayer you always hear about, then you must remain open and honest about who you are so God can fill you up with who He is.

If you have been feeling disconnected from God, reflect on how you have been approaching prayer. Have you been completely honest and forthcoming? Have you come face-to-face with the person in the mirror, even when it makes you uncomfortable? If you haven't, your lack of vulnerability may be the reason for your disconnect.

The truth is, *God will remove His veil only when you remove your mask.*

Vulnerability in prayer does not mean God wants you to *boast* in your weaknesses. He wants you to *admit* to your weaknesses so that you will not *define* yourself by them. Admitting your shortcomings is a way to release yourself back to God, so He can re-establish who you are in Him. Humility is so important to God because He knows your life can be easily corrupted by pride, which can subsequently sever your connection and extinguish your fire.

If you are stuck with knowing how to pray, the answer is to lead with vulnerability. Here are three practical ways to approach God in prayer:

1. Lead by *acknowledging* God for who He is and expressing your genuine gratitude unto Him (Psalm 100:4).

2. *Admit* your shortcomings so that they will not define you.

3. Close with an *ask,* as this creates an expectation for God to meet and exceed. Asking helps establish your faith.

A deep connection with God truly starts with an *intentional conversation*. You can always determine the health of any relationship through its communication. Whether you feel near or distant from your significant other depends on the *frequency* of your communication. God is always close, with or without prayer, but your sense of connection is solely dependent on your responsibility to communicate with Him *regularly*. Scripture 1 Thessalonians 5:17 supports the statement, *"Pray without ceasing."* The same way you keep in contact with your friends or loved ones through texting, social media, phone calls, and so forth is the same consistent engagement God desires to have with you.

It is possible you already understand the importance of prayer and how to conduct prayer. However, your disconnect from God may be tied to your lack of desire to pray. The lack of desire also comes from not fully understanding God's purpose for prayer. Many people believe prayer is for their benefit, to make requests, or to give God updates. However, prayer is not only for *you* to have access to God, but His way to have access to you! Sometimes, our approach to prayer can be one-sided, just as in the intimacy we expect in our relationships. We get so distracted by what we *feel* or *want* but not what is *necessary*. Did you know prayer is for protection and preservation? Prayer is your way to preserve your relationship with God and His way of protecting you. That is why it is important to consistently check in with God and keep the lines of communication open.

Frankly, sometimes, it is not what *you* need to say to God but what *He* needs to say to you. He wants to listen, but He also wants to speak. How often do you call people just to hear them talk and let them ramble? In most instances, rarely. You call with the intent of being heard, not solely with the intent of listening. With God, He desires both – to hear from you and to speak to you. Maybe you do not have anything to say, but God still wants to talk to you. Have you ever considered that? Prayer is not just for your pleasure, but it brings pleasure to God, too. To be clear, intimacy was not designed for the sole purpose of pleasure but *productivity*. True intimacy causes you to be fruitful. Pleasure is the byproduct of intimacy, not the goal; the goal is to produce. The productivity you desire is a result of *healthy engagement* with God.

God does not desire to be in communication with you only for the sake of talking but for the sake of *agreement*. To be in agreement means to be on one accord, as in one in heart and one in mind. For example, openly communicating with your spouse allows them to lovingly disclose your patterns, behaviors, and attitudes that have not been conducive to the relationship or person you aspire to be. From that conversation, you gain an awareness that hopefully inspires you to take ownership and adjust where applicable. Through this transparent relationship, you have given your spouse permission to hold you accountable to the standard in which you are called to live by, as well as within the boundaries of that relationship. This preserves the harmony and peace in the relationship with your spouse, as well as the relationship with yourself.

The same is applicable in prayer with God. Consistent communication with God allows Him to reveal attitudes of your heart and behaviors that do not reflect the nature of the relationship He desires to have with you. Prayer keeps you in agreement with the mind and heart of God while identifying areas within you that do not reflect His heart and mind. To remain in agreement, you must stay open to hearing what God has to say while remaining humble and objective. Communicating with God through prayer is less about being heard and more about growth, trust, and wisdom. Prayer opens the door for self-reflection and correction, all for the purpose of making you greater and better! If you want to be fruitful, you must listen to what God has to say about you to know what changes are necessary to make.

Friend, it is time to let your guard down so you can let God in! Do you desire to activate His power in your life? If so, your confidence, productivity, and performance will surely increase because intimacy with God always produces!

Respect

Though prayer is best described as *talking* with God, worship is best described as *walking righteously* with God. Worshipping shows a *healthy* relationship with the Lord. Worship is your way of telling God, "I love You, and I respect You. Thank You." You demonstrate your love and appreciation with respect through your *lifestyle*. Your lifestyle should reflect an attitude of regard – affections of admiration with an act of submission. The way you live expresses how you *feel* about God. Since you love God, you must respect Him. His Word says, *"Those who accept my commandments and obey them are the ones who love me"* (John 14:21). Your act of worship is a demonstration of your love.

Love requires a response, not just with God but in any relationship. When someone loves you, your natural response is to show them love in return. You consider them by matching their efforts, remaining loyal, and trying your best to put them before yourself (Philippians 2:3-4). God wants to be loved in the same way! He wants you to put Him first.

What does "putting God first" mean?

It means denying yourself from your natural desires and temptations. Denying yourself for the sake of the relationship is *selfless*. Respect is being selfless. It is honoring someone above yourself and considering them in your actions and attitudes. As respect relates to God, it is best illustrated in your behavior, attitudes, and interactions with other people by showing them the same grace, mercy, and kindness God shows to you. You are paying His love forward. Ultimately, this kind of respect for God helps form your *identity*. God wants you to take on His identity! That is how you worship God. Your lifestyle should reflect the very nature of God. Worship is walking righteously with God, not walking perfectly. He knows you are only human, but your desire to honor Him in the way you live is the greatest expression of love.

Perhaps you struggle with properly worshipping God because it is difficult to identify with Him, and you can't see Him. It may be hard for you to take on the character of God when you see Him as a distant and invisible deity. This view of God will naturally affect how you live for

Him – distant and disregarded. If God seems to be a figment of your imagination, you may find yourself attaching to people or things that *are* visible and seem greater than you. You will eventually take on the identity of what you *see* and admire instead of being transformed by your *faith*, but the truth is, it is hard to worship God when you are not *intentionally* trying to see Him as the Great I Am. Jesus allowed Himself to see the greatness of God, and He began to emulate it. He took on the identity of God because He recognized and appreciated God. If you are wondering why you are not productive or producing, consider how you are *walking*. When you walk like God, you produce like God. He is the Creator. He creates, and you should, too! When you focus on being like God, you will not have a problem producing. Emulate Him because you love Him and respect Him. That is the highest form of admiration.

***

Smothering the Flames – Sin

Maybe you get up every morning and pray, read your Bible, and try your best to worship God, but the fire is still missing. You have yet to see progress in your attitude, motivation, and spiritual life. You are going through the motions, and you start to wonder if the spiritual commitment is worth the effort. You don't feel any signs of God's presence, let alone a fire.

I can relate.

At one point, I was there, too.

I wondered if something was wrong with me because I would pray and then pray harder, but I could not connect. I didn't feel anything. I was officially spiritually apathetic (spiritually burned out), until one day, I was listening to Pastor Steven Furtick's sermon on the "Haunted Heart." His message on hidden sin helped me realize I was harboring feelings in my heart that caused me to be disconnected from God's presence. Isaiah 59:2 shares, *"It's your sins that have cut you off from God. Because of your sins, he has turned away and will not listen anymore."* That verse does not say you are cut off from His love, but you are cut off from His presence. Sin severs you from the fire, which is God's presence. If you are staying connected to God, you are disconnected from a *lifestyle* of sin. This does not mean you will not make mistakes. This simply means sin does not control your day-to-day life. Sin has not corrupted your life to the point that it has become your lifestyle.

Do you know what keeps a fire going?

Oxygen keeps a fire going.

Oxygen gives *life* to the fire, and it also helps a fire *grow*.

God is your oxygen, the very breath you need to keep the flames going and growing. When you disconnect from Him, how will you receive the oxygen you need?

You won't.

You can't.

Your environment starts to have more control over the life of the fire, but as you know, apart from God, there is no life, which means there won't be any fire. Now, what do you think puts out a fire? Your first guess might be water, as it was my first guess, but the quickest and most effective way to stop a fire is to *smother it.* When I put out my favorite candle, I simply put the lid on it, and the fire immediately disappears. The same is true with sin. When you *deliberately* sin, you are putting a lid on your fire. Sin smothers the fire because it contaminates the fuel and flame. It does not matter how much you cry out to God if you are still enjoying your sin.

I have prayed to God too many times to count, asking for His forgiveness and grace, but as soon as I got off my knees in prayer, I was right back in the sin that knocked me on my knees. It was an emotional rollercoaster that ruled my life for several years. I could not understand how I could cry out to God, knee-deep in tears, but rise to my feet and pursue the same chaos that brought nothing but confusion to my life.

Friend, take it from me – it is impossible for a fire to burn where the storms of sin constantly rage in your life. Trust me, I have lived that life, and it did not bring me any closer to my destiny. My sin separated me from God and my purpose because I was left with the disgrace of guilt and shame. I did not feel worthy of going after the dreams God gave me. Those two destructive thoughts interfere with growth of any kind, especially relating to your purpose and relationship with God. You must disconnect from the sin that keeps you disconnected from God.

Confession

Let's say you admit there is sin in your heart. Although you admitted to this sin, have you confessed your sin to the Lord? Confession is admission to your wrongdoings *against* God. Admitting it to yourself is simply acknowledging you fell short of *your* standard. There is a substantial difference. Confession is a result of humility, which ultimately leads to repentance and restoration. Confession is the beginning of reconciliation, freedom, and the rekindling of your fire.

Replaying your shortcomings in your mind only reminds you of the sin. It does not pardon you from it. Your pardon and forgiveness come from God. His forgiveness is immediate, and His grace is eternal. However, when you refuse to confess, you are refusing peace. The Bible says, *"When I refused to confess my sin, my body wasted away, and I groaned all day long"* (Psalm 32:3). David, the writer of this Psalm, understood that the consequences of his guilt affected more than his mind, but his physical body, too.

David was silent to confession but not to sorrow. Sin smothers the fire in you and rages *within*. Sin has a way of piercing through your heart and zapping your energy. If you know you have failed but refuse to confess, you are refusing more than His forgiveness. You are refusing His strength, grace, confidence, and so much more. If you stay severed, how can you stay strong? David continues in his distress in the next verse: *"Day and night your hand of discipline was heavy on me. My strength evaporated like water in the summer heat"* (Psalm 32:4). God's hand is extremely helpful when it uplifts, but His hand can feel awful when it presses down. Though the sin is heavy on its own, God intentionally adds more pressure on you, so you can get to the end of your pride and frail strength to call out for Him. That flickering flame you are experiencing is a result of low oil. The oil of God's mercy and grace overflows, but your unwillingness to reach for more oil through confession will cause the fire to go out.

Friend, there is no life in your refusal.

Confess now so your relationship with God can be revived, and you can move forward with peace. Do not allow your sin to smother you from God's grace, His fire, and your destiny. The time has come to take the lid off and keep it off. You have work to do!

***

Now that you fully understand that a true connection to God is more than activity but a means of activation, your newfound understanding should change your approach and focus. I mentioned earlier that staying connected is the hardest part of self-discipline, but this practice and connection are where the fire is found. If you are in pursuit of purpose, this is the foundation of the life you need to accomplish your goals. Do not overlook this part because if you do, you will miss the opportunity to ignite an everlasting fire that produces confidence, courage, consistency, and a closeness to God you can be proud of. If needed, reread this chapter as often as possible. Highlight passages and take notes, whatever you need to do to apply these spiritual principles to your life. To hear is not enough; the change is found in the doing! *Do not merely listen to the word, and so deceive yourselves. Do what it says"* (James 1:22).

Chapter Two

Perspective Is Key

How Are You Responding?

To keep the concept of perspective simple, I will share my former griev-
ance with cooking to illustrate how the mind can affect any task, big or
small. Though it may seem insignificant, it is a great example of how you
should not approach any of your endeavors, from cooking to writing
reports to budgeting expenses to going to work. As for me, serving my
family through my domestic responsibilities, specifically cooking, was a
constant thorn in my side. The kitchen was my least favorite room in my
house, but most of my time was spent there. I have never been a fan of
cooking, but my family needs to eat. My husband's cooking IQ does not
extend beyond store-bought cookies and a box of Fruity Pebbles, and my
seven-year-old can barely pour syrup on his pancakes without making a
mess. So, Mama's gotta get the job done. However, that does not mean

I looked forward to cooking. Nearly every day, I dreaded going into the kitchen. Breakfast, lunch, and dinner never seemed to stop showing up, and my boys never stopped feeling hungry. I complained so much that I bought into the idea I was nothing more than a glorified housekeeper, and cooking was a part of the job, done out of duty and not out of love. I felt guilty for dreading the responsibility of caring for the most important people in my life, but the truth is, I was not happy about cooking, and my unhappiness showed. My attitude was revealed in my approach and the meals I prepared. These meals were good, but they could have been great. When your perspective is off, you will not perform at your best. You will perform to your attitude.

Perspective is less of *what* you see and more of *how* you see it. The way you view something will cause you to form an idea or attitude toward that something. You see, your perspective can make any task feel like an assignment from Heaven or a chore from hell. Perspective can feel like a collision of reality and responsibility, which can create emotional conflict, depending on your focus. I eventually stopped focusing on the reality of not enjoying cooking, and I shifted my focus to my responsibility of caring for my family. Because of that mental shift, I was able to show up for my family with a positive attitude, performing at my best.

Perhaps you are not performing at your best because you have an issue with perspective. Well, you are reading this book because you have goals you want to accomplish, and, like me, you may dread doing the work. This is what I had to learn: Your reality does not excuse your responsibility. You must respond to the responsibility, not the reality of what you dread. Having a positive perspective can be extremely tricky because it forces you to respond to what you see or do with optimism, regardless of how mundane, tedious, or uninspiring the work may feel. Here is the truth – *you are required to do the tasks you do not enjoy in order to get things done.* Meaning, enjoyable or not, the work must get done for you to achieve your goals.

It does not matter if your goals consist of a healthy lifestyle change, starting a business, or going back to school – you are responsible for doing whatever is required to accomplish those goals. However, many fail at completing the task because of *how* they start. *Your perspective will determine your effort.* If a task seems daunting and long, you may put it off to another day, sometimes never approaching that task at all. This is when you adopt an attitude of procrastination. If you refuse to respond with optimism to your responsibility, you have made the goal a burden instead of a blessing. Think about how you have been responding to your responsibilities lately. Your response will reflect the *quality* of the work you produce *or* if you do anything at all.

Some people are at a standstill in their pursuit of purpose because they refuse to respond *appropriately.* Maybe you want to go back to school but dread the process of retrieving old transcripts, applying for financial aid, and meeting with an academic advisor. Perhaps you have been wanting to write a book but cannot get past chapter two because you dread the process of researching your topic or prioritizing time to sit and write. If you continue to avoid these responsibilities, you will continue to avoid the success you want.

I have been guilty of that, too.

While writing this book, there were days I dreaded doing the work because I knew what was required of me. So, some days, I missed the mark. When I did not respond appropriately, I did absolutely nothing. The sentiment of dread *immediately* destroyed my productivity. Dread delays progress. In fact, dread delays your destiny. Your destiny is determined by your progress. Subsequently, your progress is determined by your productivity. If you notice a start-and-stop pattern in your productivity, evaluate your attitude. Do not limit this concept to loftier tasks. This applies to your chores at home – laundry day, washing dishes, cleaning your closet, and so forth. This is where you develop the discipline that will greatly contribute to more significant and meaningful work.

I am not suggesting you cannot accomplish your goals without a positive attitude. However, I am suggesting a positive attitude will help maintain your zeal, thus making the journey more enjoyable. The whole point is to accomplish your goals with an unstoppable fire, but it requires consistent effort and a positive attitude.

You cannot run from this truth: With purpose comes responsibility, and responsibility requires a positive response from you. Look at the word *respons*ibility. Directly at the root of the word is respons(e). Response means to reply or react. You react to your responsibilities by doing the work with the right attitude. That is why perspective is key! A positive perspective helps you respond appropriately and objectively.

When I was cooking for my family, did you pick up on my terrible response to my responsibility? I felt as though cooking was a nightmare because of how I was responding. What matters is the attitude, not the task. Dread will cause your fire to die. Your fervor for your goals will be lost in the fire of a jaded perspective. To keep your enthusiasm, you must be mindful of how you respond to the work. Ask yourself:

Why am I not excited about this task?

What is it about the work that makes me want to stop?

Am I going to let a bad attitude interfere with accomplishing my goals?

What is more important – complaining about the work or completing the work?

Have I lost sight of the goal due to my attitude?

How will I feel if I stop now?

How will I feel after I complete this task?

When you ask yourself these questions, you immediately self-reflect, identify the root of your pessimism, and refocus your energy toward completion instead of complaining. Complaining never solves the problem. Complaining only creates more problems. Each week, I challenge you to ask yourself these questions to gauge your attitude and hold yourself accountable to your goals.

If this principle remains difficult for you to accept, please grasp this truth: Perspective is not about your attitude toward the work. It is about your attitude toward the *One* who told you to do it. The Bible says, *"Work with enthusiasm, as though you were working for the Lord rather than for people"* (Ephesians 6:7). No matter the goal, you are to work with *enthusiasm*, as if you were working for God, not an audience, your family, supervisor, or yourself. Enthusiasm is another word for zeal, fire, and excitement. God wants you to work with enthusiasm because He knows this is how you will perform at your best. He wants your best through all your endeavors. God is the Boss of all bosses, and He expects excellence from you. In the same way you submit to your authority in the workplace, submit your attitude, and work unto God. You will go further when you operate in excellence and enthusiasm.

Operating in the spirit of excellence will increase your productivity and performance because the focus will shift from your feelings of resistance to responding appropriately to the Lord. When pleasing God becomes the focus, more than a feeling of dread, you will be set in motion to accomplish more. That is because your intention has shifted to honoring God more than your feelings. Responding to God often looks like *action with the right attitude.* If He has entrusted you with the responsibility of any task, do the work unto Him!

Switch It Up!

Do you ever find yourself kicking and screaming while completing a task? The work eventually gets done, but have the mental beatings you took in the process become exhausting? You know you must do the work but are you burned out before you start? You are burned out because your fire is connected to your perspective. Your work should not be emotionally draining before you start. As a result, your low, unattached energy will show up in what you produce, like the outcome of my mediocre meals. The quality of your work is found in the quality of your thinking.

I want to share a very practical tip that helped me respond to my responsibility more positively: I started to do the same tasks *differently.* My reaction changed from dread to enjoyment by making small adjustments. This included, but was not limited to, my domestic *and* professional responsibilities. I had to figure out a way to do the same things every day, but with a different approach. I had to *switch it up!*

The work may never be enjoyable and won't always look like the end goal; however, the work must be done to finish your task. Circling back to my cooking example – I had to learn how to enjoy my time in the kitchen to destroy the dread that kept me defeated daily. I started to blast my favorite iTunes playlist to change the energy I was feeling. Listening to my favorite music made a huge difference in my attitude because I was able to enjoy something amid what I thought was an unpleasant task. Pleasure is not the goal, but if you can find small ways to make adjustments to improve your attitude, do it. Maybe music is not your thing or not realistic since you work in a cubicle alongside other employees. Perhaps, as you prepare for your next presentation, use voice notes to record instead of writing your notes. Maybe you can switch up the energy in your office by lighting your favorite candle or working remotely at a local coffee shop. Subtle changes can make a significant impact on your mind and how you perform your tasks. I encourage you to figure out different yet practical ways to switch up how you approach your tasks so that you will not get stuck in the mindset of dread. Flexibility and adaptability are necessary for your productivity. If you keep finding yourself stuck in dread, then perhaps it is time to figure out ways to adjust the work to your attitude.

Unfortunately, life includes routine, and there is no way around that, and it is no different from the work you must do. If you are anything like me, I dread redundancy, but since you cannot get away from routine, you must be creative in how you complete your daily tasks. If your goals consist of a fitness transformation, you will have to exercise, but that does not mean your workout has to be the same, day in and day out. Switch it up! Your goals may require you to sit in a quiet space for hours, but that does not mean your tomorrow has to look like today.

While writing this book, I had to change my environment, so I would not get sucked into an attitude of boredom. I made sure I ventured into different places in my home that did not invite a nap (the quickest way to run from responsibility) or sit idly in front of the television. I would go to our neighborhood park or the pool to change the scenery. Those examples may seem unremarkable to you, but those changes worked wonders for me because I initially wrote from my bed. I fought against the attitude of needing more sleep versus the need to write this book. You may have to fall in love with boredom and repetition because that means you are falling in love with the process. The process of building something is not always exciting, but if you do the work, the results *will* come. If the work is boring or tedious, remind yourself of the greater good and the greater God you are doing it for.

"Once I finish this project, I will be able to help thousands of people across the world!"

"Completing this degree will position me for a promotion and open doors of greater opportunity in my career."

"This workout will help me reach my fitness goals and get into that swimsuit I wanted to buy!"

Remember, the sacrifice never compares to the reward of what is to come. Small changes can make a huge difference in performance and productivity. A monotonous routine or bad attitude can threaten your purpose, and burnout will not be too far behind.

You Can Do Hard Things

I never said perspective would make the work easy, but a positive shift in your perspective will give you the right attitude to do the work. Sometimes you may question your abilities, especially when met with resistance. When the journey gets tough, you may see those challenges as opportunities to talk yourself out of completing your goal. When things go wrong, you may take it as a sign to give up. When people do not support or validate what you are doing, you may feel that you are not good enough. So many times, you allow challenges to determine whether you are cut out for this journey. I want you to understand that perspective is the gap from where you are to where you want to be. When I was stuck in the gap of frustration with my cooking, I started to believe I could not so much as recreate the recipes I found on Pinterest. I made this task more difficult than it was, even though I had the instructions in front of me. I went from not enjoying cooking to believing I was not a good cook. Your perspective is powerful. It will affect your attitude toward the work as well as the attitude toward *yourself.* The way you see your current abilities and circumstances will be the bridge to achieving your goals or a wall preventing you from crossing over. Your perception is based on what you *believe.* If you believe your goal is too hard to reach, it will be too hard to reach. If you believe you can complete the most challenging of tasks, you will complete them. It does not matter how many people encourage you and pat you on your back – if you do not believe you are capable, you will not accomplish your goals.

Your perspective is powerful because it determines your posture and then your position. If you have the posture of *determination* in the face of difficulty, you will be in a position for success. The Bible states you can do all things through Christ who gives you strength (Philippians 4:13), and what I realized is that *all* things consist of *hard* things, too. Stop talking yourself out of your dreams and goals because they are hard. They are *supposed* to be hard! Remember, purpose is not just about *producing something.* Purpose involves producing *something in you,* too. Handling difficulties requires a mental strength that goes beyond affirmations and trickles into the land of *declarations.* A declaration is a powerful, *positive* statement that *expects* to see what has been said. For example, the declaration for a person on a fitness journey would look something like this: "I will lose ten pounds and fit into my favorite pair of jeans in two months." Perspective should align with your *expectations*, not your excuses and emotions. That person may not enjoy working out, but their declaration has given them authority over their emotions.

You must walk in your authority.

When you make a declaration before you start your work, you set a positive attitude in motion, and your positivity creates the right conditions to follow. This type of statement will shift your mindset and prepare you for the work you need to do, no matter how difficult the task. Making a declaration reminds you of the authority you have over your mind, goals, and abilities. This simple gesture will re-energize your focus and work wonders for your productivity. Completion starts with a mental conversation. Every day, I dare you to declare you are capable through Christ and the perfect person for the challenge.

Just Choose!

How many times have you decided to pursue a certain idea but second-guessed yourself because a second, equally amazing idea arose? Then, instead of pursuing either idea, did you "wait on God" to tell you which you should do first?

For years, that was me. I felt like I had a treasure chest full of ideas, but I wasted so much time asking God for signs or to shout from the Heavens, "ERICKA, WRITE THE BOOK!" I did not understand how this deceptive tactic had me stalling instead of waiting. Waiting is connected to an expectation. Stalling means to be at a complete standstill, procrastinating, or doing nothing, which is exactly what I did – nothing. I stopped engaging. I stopped pursuing my goals because I wanted to know which goal to work on first. Talk about burnout! This is a result of deception.

If your perspective is off, you are a target for deception because you are misinterpreting the truth. The truth is, God does not care what you choose, at least not in the way I thought He did. He cares about you doing the work *with* Him by faith, not by sight, signals, and signs. Faith is what pleases God, and that should be your focus. I realized I adopted an attitude of procrastination, which destroyed my fire of confidence. If you notice the consequences of waiting have resulted in a lack of confidence and a complete standstill in your pursuits, then you have been deceived, too. You are not waiting. In fact, you are stalling, and *you* need to choose.

In the Book of Ecclesiastes, there is a scripture I was reminded of when I was stuck trying to choose which goal I should work on first. I hope this scripture helps you, too: "*Sow your seed in the morning, and at evening let your hands not be idle, for you do not know which will succeed, whether this or that, or whether both will do equally well*" (Ecclesiastes 11:6).

I finally decided to write this book *and* finish my other projects *with* God. I believed He would reveal the next steps after I took the *first* step toward accomplishing these feats. I changed my attitude with some *action*, and that, my friend, is what God cares about. When you act by faith, the clarity eventually comes because of your engagement, not your intellect. A fire cannot survive when there is no activity, and if you think you are waiting to hear from God, know He is waiting on you to move.

Fear Is a Perspective

In the next chapter, I will share the necessity of addressing your fears. However, you must understand that fear is a result of *perspective*. That is why perspective is key! Your fire comes from God, but it remains ablaze by you – the way you think and your attitude.

The enemy will use deception to talk you out of pursuing your goals but understand this – the enemy is not always the devil; the enemy can be your insecurities, otherwise known as your "inner me." I thought my humility kept me waiting before the Lord, but the whispers from my "inner me" were making me stall. Here is what I had to learn about stalling: I stalled because I failed to believe. Worse, *I believed I would fail.* In this case, fear was the root of my stalling. I believed I would choose wrong, so I refused to do anything. I misinterpreted the truth of God caring about my work to God choosing which work I needed to do *out of fear.*

If you minimize your perspective to what you *see*, you miss the opportunity to accomplish more than you could imagine. Many leaders have failed to communicate that fear is a matter of *perspective* - the attitudes you have drawn based on your *belief.* I want you to understand and believe this: Fear is what you perceive about yourself, your circumstances, and your opportunities. You *can* overcome fear if you change the way you think.

Fear does not feed on facts to survive. Fear is nourished by your belief. The great news is you can starve your fears by making mental adjustments. That is why perspective is key. Perspective can change the entire trajectory of your life!

If you are tired of going in a lateral direction and never seeing much progress in reaching your goals, examine your thought-life. Perhaps you will notice a lack of optimism and traces of fear and dread that resulted in a poor response to your responsibilities. The Bible says as a man thinketh so is he (Proverbs 23:7). If you observe your behavior, you will notice it directly reflects your thinking.

I want to leave you with this: *Responsibility* also reveals another hint in its origin – *ibility. Ibility* corresponds with "ability" as in capability. You are able and more than capable of responding and doing the work, regardless of what you feel and see. If God has given you responsibility, He has equipped you to do it. He is watching to see how you will *respond.*

Friend, please understand that your mind is powerful. Your mind can act like a torch to destroy your dreams, *or* your mind can be the fuel to push you toward your dreams. Do not neglect this concept of maintaining the right perspective. You deserve to stop riding an emotional rollercoaster while in pursuit of purpose. Today, declare that you will respond appropriately, even if the work is difficult. Be careful how you approach your goals because you will most likely execute according to your attitude, not your ability, and your fire could never withstand such unpredictable conditions.

Now get to work!

Chapter Three

Address Your Fears

Where There's Fear, There's Purpose

In the pursuit of purpose, fear is one of the biggest culprits of burnout because it extinguishes your confidence and distorts your perception to create a haze of doubt and confusion. Everyone is met with some form of fear while on their journey of purpose. In fact, as I sat to write this chapter, I was bombarded with the fear of getting "it" right. I questioned my ability to thoroughly explain the concept of fear so that it would not sound like the other books, quotes, and memes you see on your social media feed. I wanted to articulate fear's ultimate goal in the most relatable and relevant way without watering down fear or giving it any more power than we already do. But the truth is, fear is what it has always been – a tactic of intimidation that *we* give power.

In the last chapter, you learned about the tactic of deception regarding having the *right perspective*. Well, in this chapter, it is about understanding the position that fear has in your destiny. Fear is a bully meant to intimidate you from pursuing your purpose.

A bully is only a threat if you give it power. While pursuing your goals, you are your most powerful self, yet the most vulnerable at times. You see, walking in your purpose automatically gives you authority, but the journey can cause you to feel inferior. This is when you are the most critical of your abilities, circumstances, resources, and potential. Insecurities start to arise, doubts settle, and fear holds you hostage. Fear is doing its job, which is to stop you from doing yours.

If you are experiencing any of those things, I have good news for you: Your purpose is near!

Have you ever heard the saying, "Where there's smoke, there's fire"? This sentiment is the same with purpose. When there is fear, there is purpose! This signals that all your symptoms of fear are related to the gifts *inside* you. Even if you are not fully operating in your gift, the fear you experience is because your purpose is close. Your suspicions, insecurities, and images of failure are necessary for the transformation that will take place during your pursuit of purpose.

For the life of this book, I will continue to emphasize this point to you: *Purpose is not about what you produce, but what it produces in you first.* All those things you may struggle with regarding fear are meant to mold you. They are not meant to be viewed as penalties for dreaming. If your lens is clouded with images of fear and the punishment you assume it brings, you miss the opportunity to fulfill God's destiny for your life. Fear makes false predictions and presents them in ways that appear real and believable. Fear possesses fear. In fact, fear projects its own fear of your pending success on to you. It has officially flipped the script! Fear's only fear is that you win.

Come Out of Hiding

You can only win if you get in the game.

Maybe you are sitting on the sidelines, cheering everyone else on, while internally beating yourself up because you recognize your talent but have yet to move on it. Fear has told you to take a seat and clap for everyone else.

Maybe you are sitting because you have compared your talents to someone else and don't think your gifts are enough.

Maybe you are sitting because you don't think you are good enough.

Maybe you are sitting because you never realized how hiding your talents is just as bad as squandering them.

If the Bible is your standard for living, it must also be your sounding board when dealing with fear.

Do you remember the story about the rich master who *entrusted* his servants with a certain number of talents (money) to invest according to their abilities? Matthew 25 records this story, and I will do my best to summarize:

One of the servants was given five bags of silver, another was given two bags of silver, and the last servant was given one bag of silver. Once the master returned from his trip, he wanted to know how these men used his money. The man with the five bags invested and earned five more. The man with two bags earned two more. The master was pleased with them. He was full of praise and said, *"Well done, my good and faithful servant. You have been faithful in handling this small amount, so now I will give you many more responsibilities"* (Matthew 25:21). When the master went to the servant who was left with one bag, the man replied,

"I was afraid I would lose your money, so I hid it in the earth." The master grew angry and said, *"You wicked and lazy servant… To those who use well what they are given, even more will be given, and they will have an abundance. But from those who do nothing, even what little they have will be taken away"* (Matthew 25:26,29).

This parable reflects the same disappointment God has when you hide your talents. Your excuses will never stand up against God. If your reasons are based on comparisons, remember that the scripture clearly states that the master gave the servants their talents according to *their abilities.* God knew exactly how to proportion everyone's gifts. He knew exactly how much *you* could handle according to the way He designed *you.* No matter how great or small you think your talent is, it is never so insignificant that hiding it is the answer. You must put your talents to use.

It has been said that comparison is a thief of joy, but comparison is also a thief of *purpose.* God expects you to be faithful over whatever He has entrusted unto you. God gave you your talent so you could multiply it!

Have you ever had an idea and, sometime later, looked up and saw someone else had the exact idea, but they executed it while you were still thinking? It's like they took it and ran with it. Did you beat yourself up and say, "I thought of that years ago! That could have been me. That is *supposed* to be me!"

If you have experienced seeing your dream become someone else's reality, you must know it is because God will not waste a vision. In the same chapter listed above, the scriptures go on to tell us that God will take what you did not use and give it to someone else: *"Take the money from this servant and give it to the one with the ten bags of silver"* (Matthew

25:28). He gave it away to the person He could trust to do something with it. Can God trust *you*?

How are you unfaithful?

What has God specifically told you to do, but you've hidden your gift out of fear?

Are you supposed to start a business or write a book?

Are you supposed to earn a certification in your trade?

Are you supposed to follow your passion?

What are you neglecting to do?

Perhaps you have buried your dream so deep into fear that you do not have the slightest idea of how to dig it out. The solution is simple: *Dig by faith*. Fear encouraged you to tuck it away, but faith will help you find it and explore its possibilities. You just need to believe.

Friend, you must honor your responsibility, no matter how big, small, or scary it seems. Be faithful with what God has given you. Do not take this lightly. It angers God when He sees you hide your talents instead of honoring them. Don't you want to hear, "Well done, my good and faithful servant"? If so, then it is time to come out of hiding.

Complacency

It is possible you do not realize you have been hiding because you have become complacent, and it is even more possible you do not realize you're in a state of hiding at all.

The logic behind complacency is, "I have security. I am safe. I won't get hurt. I won't be embarrassed. Those are just silly dreams. I'm happy."

The mentality behind complacency is tricky. You think you are content and secure only because you are naïve to the dangers of playing it safe. However, the Bible challenges that thinking: *"and the complacency of fools will destroy them; but whoever listens to me will live in safety and be at ease, without fear of harm"* (Proverbs 1:33).

Wow!

Do you understand that?

You are destroying yourself when you play it safe! Your confidence unravels. Your peace is disrupted. Your faith is severed. To you, there are no *perceived* interruptions, risks, and setbacks when living a life of complacency. However, contrary to that thinking, every day is a setback because a life without a sense of urgency for purpose will be interrupted with subtle regret, unexplainable frustrations, and contempt for those pursuing their goals and dreams.

Those emotions expose the spirit's disappointments as it grieves your negligent behavior. You will not be able to pinpoint your areas of frustration because, with the naked eye, you have a satisfying life, but your spirit will feel it.

You will start to feel uncomfortable, even in your comfort zone. Complacency will no longer be a place of comfort but a place of complaint. You will find yourself complaining about your current employment, skillset, and lifestyle. What was once a place of contentment has now become a place of confusion. You will crave *more*, initially unaware of what more is. You will second-guess your relationships, job, life, and even your identity because your destiny is calling. You will hear destiny calling more and more, but in the beginning, you will not understand this sudden need for more. The feelings of unfulfillment will overwhelm you, and after you have questioned everything in your life and still can't find the answers, you will then realize the answer is *within*, that *more* lives inside you. You will search your heart, question your abilities, wonder if you are crazy, and maybe even feel alone.

If this is where you are right now, know this is a beautiful start. You are right on track. This is where you transition from a life of comfort to a life of calling. You realize you were chosen for more, and now you must pursue it. However, comfort will continue to call out to you, too. You will experience a mental tug-of-war of comfort, fighting for your attention. Comfort will convince you to be still and not ruffle any feathers, using your fears against you to keep you immobile. However, your calling will nudge your spirit, boasting a greater need to pursue your purpose.

Complacency is extremely loud, making it difficult to hear the soft nudges of destiny. The way you silence the noise of complacency is by committing to a goal and working consistently toward the goal. I cannot promise it will be easy because it will not be. The discomfort of calling will make you want to give up, but please know that comfort is another word for *regret*. You cannot reverse regret. You will live with the memories and thoughts of shoulda, coulda, woulda for the rest of your life. Some days, it will be but a whisper, while other days, it will be much louder and persistent, and you can only blame yourself.

Do not let another day pass by, forsaking the more that has been pulling at you. You have so much in you and so much in store than to sit idly in comfort because it is a sure thing. You deserve to pursue every goal and dream God has placed in your heart.

Most importantly, you must know that complacency angers God because it does not require faith. Any place that does not require you to engage your faith and trust God is dangerous. You were designed to live for Him, not yourself. God is not so much concerned with you being a success. He is more concerned with you being a *faithful steward*. Move out of complacency and utilize the gifts and talents God has given you, and wherever your gift takes you is the *right place* to be because you did it with God.

It is time to move from comfort to calling.

Analyze

When you respond to the calling over your life, it will not come without concerns. That is why it is important to address your fears. When you call your fears by name, you can destroy them. You cannot defeat something you cannot identify. Identifying your fears allows you to see them for what they really are.

Every fear has a unique purpose, all in the form of a perceived punishment. Fear will always think the worst and force you to expect the same. Here are some of the most common symptoms of fear that people face when pursuing their goals:

Insecurities of not being good enough

Fear of failure

Failing publicly

Losing money

Fear of other people's opinions (which may cause you to be a perfectionist or not to pursue at all)

Procrastination

Complacency

Jealousy

Intimidation.

Think about your current fears. Can you relate to any of those listed above?

Addressing your fears allows you to diffuse your fears. I suggest writing them down, so you can come face-to-face with your fears. Then, write the "punishment" you will experience if you ignore fear's warning signs to give up.

For example, if you are afraid of failing, ask yourself why. Is it because you are trying to prevent public humiliation or embarrassment? Pinpointing your fears will peel back the layers and get you to the root of the terror. When you come face-to-face with the worst that could happen, you free yourself from the chains of false predictions. You see, fear will always have negative predictions when it comes to your goals and dreams. It will tell you any of the following:

You are not good enough.

You can't do this.

You will fail.

People will laugh.

You will look like a fool.

Nobody will support you.

This is a terrible idea.

Those are negative predictions meant to keep you discouraged and unfulfilled. If you are fighting against those thoughts daily, then you have come to blows with fear. You are right on track. However, you cannot get stuck in those tracks, or you will continue to be unproductive.

Although fear is to be expected on your journey to purpose, it is important to note that fear is subjective, meaning many of your fears are linked to your perception of *self*. Fear will always cause you to have a skeptic's outlook about yourself, opportunities, and people. Fear can only report and support negativity because it only sees what is in the natural, limiting God's divine contribution to the reality of *your perceived limitations*. Fear focuses on what *you* have to offer, not what God has to offer. Fear removes God and His power from the equation, forcing you to rely on yourself.

This is most likely the root of your current struggles with fear – you are looking at *yourself* way too much. You are at the center. Think again about all the statements you have rooted in fear:

"I will fail."

"I will look like a fool."

"I can't…"

"I"

"I"

"I"

"I" is at the root of your fear. If your belief does not go beyond yourself, it will be impossible to move forward with courage. The truth is, you could fail, you probably are not "good enough" according to the world's standards, and you most likely would look like a fool, but here is the kicker – you *will* only fail *if you don't*. You *will* fail and look foolish *if you do not* pursue your purpose with faith and trust in God. If you do not have faith, failure is likely, which results in fear's predictions becoming your reality.

Your purpose is not about your individual effort. Purpose is about being in *partnership* with God. Purpose has less to do with your ability and more to do with His anointing. When you address your fears, you can soberly reposition yourself under God's authority and power. This repositioning will immediately remove the unnecessary pressures you have placed on yourself, making you less concerned about what you do or do not have to offer. The unrealistic expectations you had before will fall away as you rely on God's strength and all *He* has to offer. When you trust God, your trust puts you in alignment with God and makes you more aware of His faithfulness than your flaws.

Many people fail to realize that though it appears as if fear is "protecting" you, fear is actually a narcissistic tactic to protect your ego. When you operate in fear, you refuse to risk ruining your reputation for the sake of purpose. But trust me, operating in fear is not a defense mechanism against failure. It is a defense mechanism against *faith*.

Fear reacts to your thought process. Whatever you focus on will keep you in alignment or take you out of alignment. If you are experiencing overwhelming fear, it is safe to say you are out of alignment and have relied too heavily on yourself. Shift the weight of that pressure onto God, whose grace is sufficient to empower you to do great things. This is important to know – purpose is not about doing the work by your might or power; purpose can only be accomplished through His Spirit (Zechariah 4:6).

I say this with Godly love – it is not about you! I am not implying every fear is rooted in ego because I am aware that the enemy wants to kill, steal, and destroy your confident hope in God and deter you from the calling over your life. However, it is important to reflect and make sure your gaze is on the Lord's sufficiency and not your own.

Strategize

As previously mentioned, fear is a bully, and the only way to silence a bully is to show up and be brave.

In this case, bravery is not about your physical stature. It is about your *spiritual stance*. Fear can be conceived by you alone, but fear cannot be destroyed by you alone. It must be done in the Spirit. Fears can only be dismantled by the sword of the Spirit, the Word of God (Ephesians 6:17), which is an activation of your faith. Faith disarms fear. It demolishes the lies of fear with God's *truth*. Nothing can stand against God's truth. However, faith does not make fear disappear. Instead, faith makes fear *ineffective*.

Interestingly, fear is faith but in reverse. They are both a belief in something. *Fear is a belief in the worst, while faith is a belief in the best.* You can only overcome fear by succumbing to faith. You must understand this principle – when you surrender to faith and trust that God has all the details figured out, fear submits unto you. You have put fear in its proper place – beneath you!

God said, *"I have given you authority to trample on snakes and scorpions and to overcome all the power of the enemy; nothing will harm you"* (Luke 10:19).

Isn't that amazing?!

You do not have to fear because God has given you authority over *all* things, including the enemy. Remember, fear thinks in terms of punishment, but when you are called by God, you have access to the privileges of faith.

The privileges of faith consist of being courageous, confident, and more than a conqueror. By faith, you win! Per God's Word: *"Nothing will harm you"* (Luke 10:19). That is why reading the Word of God is your faith strategy. It enables you to walk with courage and authority in the face of your biggest fears. God's strength and confidence are activated in your life when you take the time to read His Word.

In Chapter One, you learned that reading your Bible is a key ingredient in developing spiritual intimacy and connecting with God. Reading your Bible is also essential to developing your faith: *"Consequently, faith comes from hearing the message, and the message is heard through the word about Christ"* (Romans 10:17). Your faith is fueled by the Word, and your faith is the fuel for your fire. You cannot have one without the other. When your faith flickers, so does your fire.

So, what exactly is faith?

"Now faith is confidence in what we hope for and assurance about what we do not see" (Hebrews 11:1). Faith refuses to believe what the eyes can see. It never needs proof. Faith's focus is never on the insignificant things man requires to guarantee success, such as resources, reasoning, or self. This kind of belief disregards logic and accredits all to the Lord. Faith is confident that the goal will be accomplished, no matter what, with God's help.

As stated earlier, you have authority. You just have to walk in that authority by faith. The Bible tells us, *"God has not given us a spirit of fear and timidity, but of power, love and a sound mind"* (2 Timothy 1:7). Friend, your fear is not holy. God is always clear about what He makes readily available for you, and your fear is not one of them. In His Word, He specifically said He did *not* give you a spirit of fear but a spirit of power, love, and a *sound mind*. Your fear contradicts God's Word.

Fear is synonymous with anxiety, and the Bible tells us, *"Do not be anxious about anything"* (Philippians 4:6). When you are bombarded with fear, the accusations are contradicting, confusing, and unsettling, not reflective of a sound mind. That is fear disrupting your peace and arousing your anxiety to keep you in limbo, ultimately causing you to burn out. You break the chains of anxiety when you engage your faith.

Your faith is so necessary because your faith gives you access to God, not just to His provision but His *protection* as well. Scripture says, *"And the peace of God, which transcends all understanding, will guard your hearts and your minds in Christ Jesus"* (Philippians 4:7). The Lord will give you His peace that will *guard your mind.*

Peace is the reward of your faith.

Peace aborts the attacks of fear. You start to hear God's voice encouraging you and comforting you more than the threats of your fears. When you experience constant discouragement in pursuit of your purpose, it is because fear has attacked your *mind,* causing you to doubt yourself and the Lord, thus resulting in a lack of peace. Still, when you take heed to God's instruction to *"Lean on, trust in, and be confident in the Lord with all your heart and mind and do not rely on your own insight or understanding"* (Proverbs 3:5), God's peace will protect you *and* your burning flame as you pursue purpose.

Audacious Faith

I dare you not just to have faith, but to have *audacious* faith! I also believe God wants you to have this kind of bold faith because it forces you to believe bigger, not in yourself but in Him. A mediocre faith does not expect miracles, but an audacious faith does.

Maybe your dream does not match your reality. Your goals may seem too big to fit into your budget, sphere of influence, or your ability, but here is the thing – your faith should never be limited to your reality. That is not faith. Those are facts! God operates in an entirely different realm of possibility. With God, *all* things are possible, even that seemingly impossible dream.

The Bible reminds us, *"Jesus looked at them and said, 'With man, this is impossible, but not with God; all things are possible with God'"* (Mark 10:27). Your dream may be impossible to accomplish alone, but *with* God, it is possible! That is the idea of audacious faith. It operates only on the awareness of God's power, not your powerlessness. This kind of faith recognizes the challenge but is not negatively influenced by it. What looks like a red flag for many will look like a green light, signaling your turn to go.

Let's consider Abraham for a moment. He was without a child and so desperately wanted one. Abraham was about 100 years old when God told him He would make him a father of many. Most people would say, "How? I'm too old! How will I have many when I don't even have one?!" But Abraham's faith was audacious. He believed God, despite his reality, and because of his faith, God declared Abraham a father *before* he and his wife conceived.

Let Abraham's testimony be of some encouragement for you: *"Abraham was first named 'father' and then became a father because he dared to trust God to do what only God could do... When everything was hopeless, Abraham believed anyway, deciding to live not on the basis of what he couldn't do but on what God said he would do"* (Romans 4:17-18).

This is why it is important to have audacious faith. Audacious faith is a faith that dares to believe in the *impossible*. When you dare to believe like Abraham, you have access to God's goodness and grace, too.

Perhaps the idea of starting a business may seem ridiculous because you can barely pay your rent right now. The idea of getting your first or second degree seems foolish because you are a single mother, trying to make ends meet, or it believes you can be a New York Times bestseller with no sign of a publishing deal or literary agent, but audacious faith says, "God *can* and *will* make a way out of no way."

That is miracle thinking!

Nothing is too hard for God. After all, He is the Creator of the universe, so creating opportunities and resources for you is no big feat for Him.

Let's be clear – audacious faith is daring God to meet your *reverent* expectation with His supernatural power. This kind of faith does not merely test God's authority, but it acknowledges and honors God's authority. Your request is *respectfully* asking God to show up and produce in ways that only He will get the glory. An answered prayer is not an opportunity for you to parade around and boast in your doing. Instead, your accomplishment should direct everyone's attention to the faithfulness of God. When you dare to believe big with that kind of integrity, the Bible says, *"Because of your faith, it will happen"* (Matthew 9:29).

It doesn't matter how big your dream is; God's Word says, "*because of your faith, it will happen*." The scripture does not say because of your ability, finances, or network; it responds only to your faith.

Examine where your faith is right now. Is it bold and daring, or is it frail and timid? According to what you believe, it will be done. If you are only expecting a little, you will get little. If you are expecting big, you will get big. God will answer according to the size of your faith. Do not scale back on believing based on what you see because you miss opportunities for God to blow your mind. He wants to do *immeasurably* more than what you can imagine or believe. Yes, it's true, and it says it in His Word: *"Now to him who is able to do immeasurably more than all we ask or imagine, according to his power that is at work within us"* (Ephesians 3:20). Even that outrageous dream you keep replaying in your mind can be outdone.

Is your faith too practical?

Can you accomplish your dream alone?

If so, believe bigger! Dreaming is an opportunity to put your faith to the test and go on an adventure with God. No good adventure is ever limited to reality. With God, there are no limits! The Lord desires to go on an adventure with you to explore the depths of His love, your gifts, and your faith. A vision that does not require you to venture deeper with God is a missed opportunity to grow and experience His glory like never before.

When you have the nerve to believe God, it pleases Him. The Bible says, *"And without faith, it is impossible to please God"* (Hebrews 11:6).

Isn't that something?

It is *impossible* to please God without faith. There is nothing you can do that will please God if it is not done by faith. It brings great pleasure to God when you trust Him. He desires for you to believe.

Friend, I dare you to be bold in your pursuits!

I dare you to take a chance!

I dare you to believe for bigger!

I dare you to start again!

I dare you to believe in the impossible!

Perhaps you may feel like your purpose is intimidating, and dreaming bigger seems a bit risky, but purpose is never a risk when God orders your steps. The Bible says, *"The steps of a good man are ordered by the Lord, and He delighteth in his way"* (Psalm 37:23). It does not matter if no one understands your journey or if it appears you are going the wrong way because the Lord has already gone before you and He will walk beside you, just as God told Joshua: *"Have I not commanded you? Be strong and courageous. Do not be afraid; do not be discouraged, for the Lord your God will be with you wherever you go"* (Joshua 1:9).

Pay attention to those words: *"Wherever you go."* It doesn't matter if your goal is local or global because God will be right there with you. He just asks that you be strong and courageous. You demonstrate your strength and courage by going forth. Faith requires action: *If you believe, you must go.* When you do what God has told you, you are displaying strength and courage in the face of fear.

Having audacious faith will, without a doubt, stir up people's opinions of you, and they may resolve to think you are in over your head with your goals and beliefs, but this would not be the first time nor the last. Imagine for a moment how foolish Noah may have looked to his friends, relatives, and community for building an enormous boat to save his family and two of each animal from a flood. That may even sound ridiculous to you. His purpose was massive. It would not be surprising if his community ridiculed him and mocked his decision to do what God told him to do. The insults and mocking he would have experienced in modern-day would probably go something like this:

Ha! He's a fool!

Build a boat to save the world?!

God chose you out of all people?

What makes him so special?

A boat?! That doesn't make sense.

The Bible does not tell us that Noah experienced that kind of backlash, but the Bible does illustrate Noah's audacious faith. Noah did what God told him to do, no matter the cost, the look of it all, or the time. Audacious faith can be offensive to the people in your life because your goals may seem too farfetched and unrealistic based on their level of faith, but their opinions do not matter. Outsiders do not have the same vantage point as you, so it will be impossible for them to see the vision the way you see it.

In that case, be like Noah. Build, hammer to nail, every day, no matter how ridiculous it may seem to everyone around you, including you. That is how you demonstrate audacious faith – you do the work anyway with strength and courage. Do not concern yourself with the whispers of others, only the voice of God. Then, you will be successful in all you do. *"You will succeed in whatever you choose to do, and light will shine on the road ahead of you"* (Job 22:28). Hold on to God's Word, even when everyone and everything around you may contradict your faith.

They Don't Matter

If you can be honest with yourself, you probably wonder things like:

Will they like me?

Will they support me?

Will they criticize me?

Will they judge me?

Will I be humiliated?

This questioning is focused on other people's judgments rather than your duty to do the work God has called you to do. You have made their projections more of a priority than your responsibility to do the Will of God.

I want you to know this truth and guard it with all your heart: *God does not protect the opinions of people. He protects the obedience of those who do what He told them to do.* You move outside of God's protection when you start fearing what people think of you.

Proverbs 29:25 warns us, *"Fearing people is a dangerous trap, but trusting the Lord means safety."* When you fear people, you put your destiny in danger. When a person is trapped, they cannot move because they are restricted to one place. The same goes for you. It will be impossible to move forward in purpose when you are trapped by your fear of man.

Are you going to let what people think of you stop you from dreaming and doing what God has called you to do?

If so, you run the risk of losing it all. You will lose the opportunity to experience true freedom, the satisfaction of completing your goals, and the reward of pleasing God by doing the work by faith.

If you have been feeling stuck because you have been bombarded with fear of people's opinions, you can immediately release yourself from that dangerous trap when you decide to trust God. Free yourself now and move forward, doing what God told you, and then you will walk in safety, even amid the chatter. When you respond with this level of trust in God, you will exemplify the true meaning of this scripture, *"So we can say with confidence, The Lord is my helper; I will not fear. What can mere people do to me?"* (Hebrews 13:6). This kind of confidence makes people's opinions ineffective because you know God is on your side.

Failure is Not an Option

If you entertain fear to the point you believe humiliation is on the other end of purpose, you are mistaken. The great thing about having audacious faith is knowing what is real and what is not. Your fear of humiliation is a waste of imagination. When you respond to God's call to live out your purpose, you could never fail because you could never quantify the rewards of obedience.

If your pursuits are from selfish ambition, then yes, you can fail because you can quantify a loss motivated by *self*. However, if your heart is pure and without selfish motives, God will not allow you to experience humiliation when you have committed to His calling over your life. His Word confirms this promise: *"Do not be afraid, you will not be put to shame. Do not fear disgrace; you will not be humiliated"* (Isaiah 54:4). Purpose could never result in shame for a person who ventured confidently into the unknown for the sake of God's purpose. Since we know purpose is being in partnership with God, you cannot fail. Let Philippians 2:13 be your reminder: *"For it is God in you to will and to act in order to fulfill His good purpose."*

Visualize

Visualizing is one of my favorite ways to disarm my fears. Visualizing takes me from where I am to where I want to be, and I would like to encourage you to do the same. In this case, positive visualization engages your imagination to see yourself as accomplished and as happy as you aspire. God has gifted you with imagination – use it in your favor!

Visualizing is your ability to see beyond what the eyes perceive to what the spirit knows. Your spirit has already met the person you are trying to be. Your spirit is your *authentic* self that does not entertain your fears. Your spirit entertains your fate. When you close your eyes to see by faith, you live your dream *before* you do the work, as if your destiny unfolds before your eyes. God tells us in Habakkuk 2:3, *"This vision is for a future time. It describes the end, and it will be fulfilled."*

How remarkable is that?

You can experience the future in the present.

You can see yourself fully operating with your gift in the authority God has given you.

There is incredible power in visualizing!

Visualizing helps eliminate your insecurities and doubts. When you experience seeing yourself reach your full potential, it confirms fear is a liar. Every time fear said you couldn't, you would fail, or you weren't good enough, your visualization destroys the images fear tried to use to stop your progress. Visualizing your goals is a powerful way to break free from your fears because you have experienced success before completing the process, and in many cases before you start. The feeling of future success will motivate you to keep going by faith.

God wants you to use your imagination.

What do you think faith is?

It is an unseen image of a real God! Your faith is a result of your imagination. God also wants you to use your imagination when operating in His purpose. His Word says to speak those things that are not as though they were (Romans 4:17). Although you have not yet achieved what you want, you must speak as if it has already been done. For example, suppose your goal is to start a photography business. In that case, you may say something like, "I am a successful photographer with my own photography studio, photographing editorial shoots with the biggest clients in fashion." You must speak specifically about what you want as if you already see it until you see it. That is visualizing by faith. Visualizing confirms your dreams are achievable, even when they seem inconceivable.

When visualizing, it is also important to pay attention to how you feel.

Do you feel excited?

Powerful?

Accomplished?

Are you smiling?

Imagine yourself from the inside out. This is key because when your fears try to discourage you, you can reflect on the emotions you experienced through your visualizations. Reminding yourself of how you will feel after achieving your goals reduces the impact on the present threats of your fears.

Although faith is key in facing fears, your visualizations support your faith. If it is difficult for you to visualize, it is safe to say there may be some unbelief blocking you from believing in your future successes. I encourage you to accept the principle of *audacious faith* and fully surrender to the truth that "impossible" is only an illusion when in partnership with God. Sometimes, your fears can be so deeply rooted that they disrupt your ability to imagine doing and being greater. However, you must be persistent in engaging your faith and mind to see beyond your current circumstances and insecurities. Visualization breaks the barriers that fear tried to place on you to explore the limitless possibilities of purpose. Once you see your purpose manifest in your mind and spirit, you become unstoppable on your journey!

Allow the *future* you to motivate the *current* you to keep going. Your momentum is connected to your ability to dream. When you lose your imagination, you lose your fire. In fact, you lose more than your fire. You lose out on fulfilling a divine destiny. The Bible says, *"If people can't see what God is doing, they stumble all over themselves, but when they attend to what he reveals, they are most blessed"* (Proverbs 29:18). If you lack vision, you will lose sight of a meaningful life. *You will stumble.* However, if you engage your imagination and commit to what God reveals to you, *you will be blessed.*

One more important takeaway of visualizing is understanding the importance of writing down your vision. The Bible is full of wonderful insight, not just for informational purposes but for application. Take Habakkuk 2:2, for example: *"Write this. Write what you see. Write it out in big block letters so that it can be read on the run. This vision-message is a witness pointing to what's coming."*

Your vision is powerful because it is evidence of what's to come. Writing the vision on paper is a form of divine confirmation that will keep you encouraged as you work toward your goal.

This is another method of canceling fear. The more you see the vision, the more you will believe you can achieve your goal. Just as a witness must write a statement for the court of law based on what they have seen, God wants you to write what you have witnessed while visualizing. You witnessed something no one else could see, and writing your vision is the *evidence* you can rely on in the face of contradicting information. Your vision statement supports the faith of your desired outcome. Your vision statement is proof in the face of fear.

Though the goal has yet to be accomplished, fear loses its momentum when you dare to engage your imagination and write it plainly. To clarify, to write plainly is another way of saying be clear. Being clear requires a concentrated effort that focuses solely on information that supports the big picture. You should write objectively and to the point. When you write your vision clearly, you can *see* it clearly. There is no confusion about your desired outcome. This practice of writing your vision will keep you energized as you run toward the destiny God set especially for you. It will be difficult for you to fear a future you can clearly see. Even when you come face-to-face with challenges on your journey, your vision will be a reminder of what is possible if you dare to dream!

Chapter Four

Respect the Process

Introduction: Preparation

This is the part of the journey where most people turn back to a life of comfort instead of pursuing a life of calling.

Why?

Because this is where many feel the pressure of the process, causing extreme discouragement and, ultimately, burnout. The process is especially difficult for those who do not understand how valuable the process is to the journey.

You may wonder, "What exactly *is* the process?" or "What's the *point* of the process?" Many minimize the process to the time it takes to achieve a goal. This is not completely wrong, but it is misleading. The process requires time, but the process is a more personal experience for anyone en route to achieving their goals. The process is a supernatural experience for those who dare to do more and be more while undergoing a transformation that challenges their character, attitudes, and commitment. To progress, you will have to come face-to-face with your bad habits, negative self-talk, and other self-defeating behaviors so that God can transform you from a person of excuses to a person of excellence. It will feel as if the changes you need to make are impeding your progress or, at the very least, slowing you down. However, the process does not disrupt you from your purpose. It *prepares* you for it.

As in any transformation, there will be a series of actions that need to take place, so you can fully develop into the person God wants you to be. That is the purpose of the process – to transform you from good to great. The transformation is not to be taken lightly, as it will apply holy pressure on you, not so you can give up, but so you can *grow up.*

Once you grasp the significance of the process, you will not only anticipate the challenges it may bring, but you will be more willing to cooperate with this divine and transformative experience. I hope to help you navigate through your journey of purpose as aware as possible so that you can respond appropriately. Take it from a woman who, for many years, did not understand the value nor the necessity of the process, which caused me to be counterproductive in my pursuits. I wasted so much time trying to get around the process, not realizing the process was mandatory to make progress toward my goals. As gifted as I thought I was, and as gifted as you may be, being gifted will never be enough to live your purpose fully. In fact, purpose is a byproduct of the process. If you skip the process, you *cannot* and *will not* fulfill your purpose. Purpose is achieved because of going through the process of tests, patience, and faith. This is what you must understand – the process is not going anywhere, and neither will you if you keep trying to avoid it. You will remain stuck, discouraged, and defeated because you believe there is a magical way around your obligation to your goals. If you want to see results, you must *respect the process.*

R-E-S-P-E-C-T

You may have heard encouraging comments such as "trust the process" or "embrace the process" as you share your frustrations on your journey to achieving your goals. Those comments suggest to passively comply without responsibility. However, those recommendations help you cooperate with the process to get the results you want. Respecting the process places responsibility on you that demands an appropriate response and action.

Respect is recognizing the worth or value of someone or something, regardless of the attitude toward that person or thing, allowing you to respond or interact maturely. The same is required for the process. You do what is necessary for the *greater good.* It does not matter if your attitude is of disdain or excitement. Your response should be one of *respect.* When you respect the process, you can *accept* the process, even when it is difficult. Through this acceptance, you recognize *your* responsibility to respond according to the desired goal, not the perceived difficulty.

Unfortunately, many people fail to respond appropriately, mainly because they were unaware of how to respond. When unequipped with the knowledge and tools to overcome self-sabotaging behaviors, setbacks, and frustrations, it only makes sense for you to keep feeling defeated and return to a life of comfort instead of calling. However, suppose you want victory, once and for all. In that case, this chapter will help you identify your weaknesses, understand the importance of character development, reignite your faith, and provide practical ways to respond to the nature of *your* process. Everyone's process is not the same, so you would do yourself a disservice to compare your journey to anyone else's journey. God designed this distinct experience for *you* to grow into *your* purpose, lacking no good thing. As I mentioned in previous chapters, the journey of purpose will always produce something in you before it can produce something from you. This is where that statement comes even more alive and becomes more relevant on your journey: *during the process.*

What will your process reveal about you?

Will it reveal a commitment to your purpose or your self-defeating habits?

My prayer is that this chapter will correct some things in your life that thwart your progress, whether sabotaging behaviors, your attitude, or a perceived lack of discipline. On the contrary, some things will be out of your control, but the goal is to maintain a steadfastness, mentally and spiritually, that will keep you on fire as you go through the fires of life.

No matter God's intent for your life, my prayer is that you will connect with what He is doing in your life so that you can move forward in the face of difficulties. After reading this chapter, I am certain you will feel equipped to handle whatever challenges may come, refueling you to go through the process and gain victory over the obstacles holding you back.

Are you ready to finally accomplish those goals? Well, the time has come to stop resisting the process and start respecting it!

Be Proactive

The process is not the time to feel discouraged and give up on the promises of God or your goals. The process is a more *intentional call-to-action*, where you respond *strategically* to every obstacle that may come your way. Perhaps you are experiencing some difficulty, causing your excitement to fizzle, or you are starting to second-guess this whole notion about having purpose. That is because the process is known to apply pressure to peel away one's superficial motivations to reveal their heart's true purposes.

What will the process uncover about you?

Were your ambitions selfishly motivated or inspired by God?

Will you fold under pressure or do whatever it takes to achieve your goals?

Depending on how you respond will reveal the truth of your intentions. If your why isn't strong enough, your work ethic won't be either.

The process is where you will face the fork in the road – left to turn back (reactive) or right to keep going (proactive). The successful ones typically choose "right to keep going" and refuse to let their feelings and frustrations deter them from their dreams and goals.

On the contrary, unsuccessful people choose "left to turn back" because they have allowed their emotions to control them. If you are currently at a fork in the road, I urge you to choose based on your destiny and not your feelings. Gifts and talents are not what sets successful and unsuccessful people apart. The distinction is whether they are *reactive* or *proactive*. Successful people are proactive, while unsuccessful people are reactive. You cannot pursue the promises of God based on your feelings.

When you are reactive, you will always react to what you see or feel, which will never lead you in the right direction. The moment you are rejected, unsupported, or experience a setback, your feelings will tell you to "Give up," "This isn't meant to be," and "You're wasting your time!" Those who reason with this kind of thinking typically use those experiences as the reason they give up. This is not to say successful people are not challenged with the same kind of taunting thoughts. However, they decide not to react with their feelings but with *action*. Reactive people succumb to their feelings while successful people overcome their feelings.

To be proactive is to respond with a solution to a problem versus a complaint. It is having the mindset of "Where there's a will, there's a way." A proactive person will always attempt to figure out how to achieve their goals, even if it means readjusting, reprioritizing, and refocusing. If you allow your emotions to determine your every move, you will surely succumb to every naysayer, challenge, insecurity, and fear on the road to purpose. You must decide you will be proactive and solution-oriented in the face of difficulty. Otherwise, you will get stuck in the problem and never accomplish your goals. Your fuel should be connected to your purpose, not your feelings, which is the surest way to lose your fire. On the contrary, when your destiny is your fuel, you will disengage from your emotions and keep your momentum for your goals through *action*. If you want to be successful, you must be proactive.

The problem with being proactive lies in knowing *how* to respond when those challenges arise. To help you on your journey of purpose, the following pages will detail the most critical stages of the process that you may perceive as problems and the proactive ways to respond to those challenges. These strategies will teach the true art of respecting the process to achieve your goals, once and for all. Most people will tell you to trust the process, but I encourage you to trust God and respect the process, as these are keys to your productivity and purpose.

Pruned for More

Often, people view purpose as a transactional experience versus a transformative one. People enter purpose with the mindset of "If I *do* this, then I should *get* that." However, purpose thinking should be, "I will *get* to that when I get *through* this." Vision can be misleading to people with transactional thinking because they expect immediate returns from their working investment. Transformative-thinking people understand the necessity of transformation and its impact on themselves, and, most importantly, their purpose. However, I have good news – no one wakes up and decides to be a transformative-thinking person without an opportunity to choose. The process presents an opportunity wrapped in adversity, leaving you to decide if you will cooperate or walk away.

Perhaps you are in the decision-making process, trying to determine if the vision is worth the pain of your transformation. You may be conflicted because your visualizations never included this dark and confusing place. Those visualizations did not hint at the challenges and frustrations you would have to encounter on your path to purpose. That is because vision will never reveal *how* it will happen. Vision only shows you that it *will* happen. The promise will be fulfilled but hardly ever in the way you imagined.

You may be thinking, "Why is this so hard? Why do I have to go through this? I should just give up! What's the point?"

Those sentiments reflect an attitude that you have been forsaken or mistreated, but the truth is, the testing of your faith and character are

73

prerequisites for purpose. You cannot be transformed if you cannot be tested. When you respond to the calling over your life, you must also respond to God's testing and pruning. Spiritual pruning is a removal and replenishment process, removing *anything* considered a threat to your destiny and replenishing more of what is necessary for it. John 15:2 states, *"He cuts off every branch in me that bears no fruit, while every branch that does bear fruit he prunes so that it will be even more fruitful."*

People have mistakenly defined pruning as a season of cutting all the "bad" things within you. However, that is only half true. The scripture states that God will cut off what is not producing. *"He cuts off every branch in me that bears no fruit"* (John 15:2), which could be some of your self-sabotaging behaviors that could hinder your effectiveness in achieving your goals. The same scripture goes on to say, *"While every branch that does bear fruit he prunes so that it will be even more fruitful"* (John 15:2). The main objective for pruning is not because you are doing anything wrong but because you are doing something right. This should encourage you! God prunes you so you can be more fruitful and effective in your calling.

Agriculturally, it is said that pruning is another way to stimulate growth and improve the productivity and longevity of plants, and the same applies to you. God does not want you to compromise your calling due to detrimental character flaws. Your purpose demands a better version of you, and it calls for the removal of old habits, negative attitudes, and behaviors. If you are struggling, mentally or emotionally, it may be a sign that God is stimulating growth inside of you. Determine what area of your life is being pruned, and it will calm your fears of feeling like you are under attack because you are really being pruned for more.

Being pruned is an opportunity to proactively respond to what God reveals to you about your current behaviors and the attitudes of your heart. God may need to cut your sense of ego, fear, low self-esteem, misplaced trust, and other character traits that could prevent you from reaching your full potential. However, the only way those traits are revealed is when you respect the process by doing the work. Pruning starts with the practical. Respecting the process is not just doing the work required for your goals. Respecting the process is also tending to the work *within so that* you can be pruned for more. If you want to start reaping, you must first understand pruning.

Practical Growth

Though the process is a supernatural experience of pruning and transformation, the experience seems to be anything but supernatural. That is because transformation happens in the daily, practical practices and routines of your life. This is where you learn where you are flawed in the process. God already knows the areas in which He wants to see growth, but the process exposes what needs to be pruned inside you. Real transformation happens as you respect the process by doing the practical things necessary to accomplish your goals. Your practical responsibilities may include research, networking, creating a marketing plan, budgeting, and scheduling, to name a few. Those tasks may seem irrelevant when it comes to your pruning experience, but trust me, those practical tasks are very revealing.

You see, I rarely find that people are frustrated in their process because they do not *know* what needs to be done. They are frustrated because they are not *doing* what they know needs to be done. You can probably

75

relate to this. Most people assume their struggle between knowing and doing is because they lack discipline or consistency, but that is not the case. Those are only symptoms of a deeper issue.

How do I know this?

Because God's Word explicitly states that He has given you a spirit of discipline, and since you have been gifted with the spirit of discipline, consistency results from activating it. Your denial does not eradicate this truth. Instead, it prevents you from *learning* the truth. Relying on these half-truths keeps you going in circles, never freeing you to become the person God intended. You have used your excuses as a crutch, so when things get challenging, you can fall back on "I'm not disciplined" without ever being accountable for your goals. The excuse of not being disciplined prevents you from discovering the *real* reason behind your unproductivity. I say this not to condemn you but to help you break free from a cycle meant to extinguish your fire for your purpose.

Pruning is a spiritual process, but God uses the things in the natural that you struggle with to shed light on the bigger problem. You have probably recommitted to your goals several times by writing a detailed plan, but you are no closer to your goals than when you first started a month ago or years ago. It is not because you do not know *how* to do what is on your to-do list. The problem is you do not know *why* you cannot seem to carry out your plan. There is a spiritual barrier preventing you from performing at your best, and without knowing the *why*, you will not complete the *what*.

For example, as I was writing this book, I realized I struggled with procrastination and poor time management. I thought acknowledging myself as a procrastinator would lessen the sting of my unproductivity.

I proclaimed, "I'm a procrastinator," as if it were a badge of honor, but really, it was my way of coping with my poor performance. I thought being a procrastinator excused me from my responsibilities because it defined what I could not seem to do. A procrastinator is a person who puts things off that should be done in a timely manner. I could identify with that! However, being a procrastinator does not explain *why* you are that way. It only explains the result of your lack of productivity. Calling myself a procrastinator allowed me to excuse my behavior, not change it. The definition does not uncover the problem. It masks it.

I also decided my poor time management was simply part of my identity. Even when I kept going back to my schedule, trying to re-prioritize my day, I struggled with productivity. No matter how many times I tried to follow a schedule, it never worked. It was because God needed to reveal *why* I struggled with managing my time properly. I eventually went to God, asking Him to reveal why prioritizing time was so challenging, and this is when things started to change for me.

He showed me my complacency.

I did not have a sense of urgency for my purpose because I was enjoying my comfort zone. It was hard to stick to a schedule I did not respect. I appeared to be serious about my calling, but my priorities proved I did not respect the process or purpose.

God also revealed that my procrastination was a result of fear. I never knew I struggled with a spirit of fear and complacency until I worked on the practical things in the natural. Your responsibility in the natural is how God reveals the work you need to do in the spiritual. This is how God partners with you in the pruning process. Because of this new knowledge, I was more aware of my behavior and intentionally started choosing my calling over comfort. Before, I thought my struggle with time management held me back, but it was my fear of failure and need for comfort. From that revelation, I was open to God's transformation, starting in my mind and subsequently changing my behavior.

I stopped calling myself a procrastinator because it justified my fear. I stopped making excuses for my poor time management because it justified my complacency. Before this revelation, I was frustrated in the process, defining my bad habits instead of overcoming them. Although I saw a manifestation of procrastination and poor time management, those were bad fruits produced from a seed of fear. I would have never identified my fear if I were not open to God's revelation.

What fruits are you seeing in your life that are slowing down your progress? I encourage you to take those things to God so that He can reveal the truth behind your perceived justifications.

For example:

You see procrastination. God sees fear.

You see the inconsistency. God sees your need for instant gratification and approval.

You see a perfectionist. God sees insecurity.

You see bad time management. God sees complacency.

You see impatience. God sees unbelief.

You see laziness. God sees apathy.

Your natural is what you see. The spiritual is what God reveals.

This is one way God stimulates your growth. You may be annoyed by what appears to be your hang-ups, but God uses them to mature you in your faith and develop your character.

What do you believe God is pruning in you?

Remember, spiritual pruning removes things that threaten your destiny and replenishes more of what helps. In my case, I realized God was pruning my faith! He had to remove what was interfering with my productivity, which was my fear, so that I could produce more out of my faith.

Today, I can confidently say I am not a procrastinator. However, when I start to see myself slip into procrastination, I know it is a sign I am being held back by fear. When I am not managing my time properly, I remember I need to value my calling. Those two examples are how God uses your hang-ups to your advantage, the advantage of seeing significant progress toward your goals and inner being. When you respect the process, you experience rewards of growth. You see, life is all about processes, and you will never get away from that. However, your experience gives you the knowledge you need to expedite your *next* process. God's revelation breeds self-awareness, which prompts better performance.

Isn't God amazing?

Even when the process is uncomfortable and frustrating, God uses discomfort for your benefit. In the end, you grow and become the person God intended.

The success of your goals is measured by the success of your pruning. Do not fight God when it seems His hand is hurting you. Understand His hand may cause pain but never without producing something beautiful. If you want to reach your full potential, you must respect the process by doing practical things so that God can unveil spiritual revelations.

You Are Disciplined

As I mentioned earlier, declaring, "I am not disciplined" is a safety net for people to avoid accountability. You will most certainly struggle with operating in discipline when the root of your problem goes undetected. Until the real problem is revealed, your broken system disguises itself as a lack of discipline. This is because discipline is difficult to correct without knowing why it is broken. Unfortunately, this is the enemy's way of keeping you stuck because if you identify as undisciplined, you deny the truth that God has given you a spirit of discipline. The enemy would much rather you walk in a broken identity instead of your God-given one. Satan rejoices every time he hears you deny the spirit God has given you.

Friend, you can't make it that easy for him!

The moment you are not operating in discipline, do not deny you have discipline. Instead, accept that you have not operated in it. The difference is that you acknowledge your ownership of the spirit of discipline while admitting to not functioning in it. Be careful never to deny yourself of what you have been divinely equipped with.

If I can be transparent with you, discipline seems like a tall order to fill because of its difficulties and pain. It feels like a constant denial of everything pleasant, comfortable, and enjoyable. Can you relate? Denying yourself in those ways seems to take the fun out of, dare I say it… life? But what is life without discipline?

Life without discipline is chaos.

Think about it. Though the discipline I am referring to is the spirit of discipline, there is also a principle of discipline with the same cause and effect. For example, if you are a parent, I am sure you discipline your child to teach them right from wrong. The discipline they receive from you *trains* them to be good little people, so they will be good big people when they grow up. Discipline is your way of correcting their bad behavior and attitudes to prevent them from operating in chaos. The same goes for you and your relationship with God. He has given you a spirit of discipline to help train you.

Discipline is what corrects your need to binge-watch television shows.

Discipline is what corrects your need to live idly.

Discipline corrects your need to ignore your responsibilities.

Your spirit of discipline is to protect you from a life of chaos! Though the order may seem tall, operating in discipline is for your protection.

The Bible states: *"No discipline seems pleasant at the time, but painful. Later on, however, it produces a harvest of righteousness and peace for those who have been trained by it"* (Hebrews 12:11).

Yes, consistently operating in discipline can be painful because discipline is resolute, unwavering, and uncompromising. You are probably thinking, "But I'm not." No, you most likely are not resolute, unwavering, and uncompromising on your own, but the spirit of discipline *trains* you to be. That is why God gifted you with discipline, so you can grow into a person who *is* resolute, unwavering, and uncompromising. Do not despise your spirit of discipline because it is uncomfortable. Welcome discipline so you can avoid the uncomfortable consequences of chaos.

Spiritual Boot Camp

Being trained requires breaking old habits and patterns and replacing the old with the new. That is the goal of discipline – training to be great. Your spiritual training will not be enjoyable, as you will have to constantly choose to do the right thing when the wrong thing seems easier. Examples include choosing faith over doubt, sacrifice over sabotage, productivity over procrastination, patience over shortcuts, and so forth. Those choices will be challenging to make at the moment, but whichever you choose exposes where you are in your training.

Your choices during training reveal if you are cooperative or resistant. For example, imagine that you started going to boot camp. When you start the program, you may feel the exercises are unnatural and difficult. You start to feel pain in your body that you have never experienced. The pain in your body starts to affect your mind. You start to become mentally fatigued and ready to find every excuse to quit. This is also what happens when you are spiritually trained. You will want to resist doing the very things that feel unnatural, but if you keep cooperating, you will notice a transformation. If you want to be a person who operates in the spirit of discipline and gets things done, you must commit to your training. In the same way an individual may envision the results of their physical training, you must envision the results of your spiritual training. The results are the same – *training gets you in shape*. Discipline is what gets you in shape, so you can be the most well-rounded and productive person you have imagined. If you want better performance, stop denying your spirit of discipline. Embrace it! The benefits will always produce optimal performance and greater productivity.

Operating in the spirit of discipline is imperative during the pruning process because it demonstrates that a well-trained person can be trusted when the cutting shears are put away. If you can deny yourself of your will, God knows you can be trusted to respond to His Will and purpose. Your development is what matters to God, not your accomplishments. Take Joseph, for example. Scripture explicitly states, *"Until the time came to fulfill his dreams, the Lord tested Joseph's character"* (Psalm 105:19). The same is true for you. *Your character must be tested so your calling can be sustained.* Your story may not be as extreme as Joseph's, having been rejected by his brothers and sold into slavery. He experienced lies and character assassination with a penalty of prison, all because God favored him. Those things happened to Joseph, not because he was a bad person, but because there was so much good in him. However, Joseph needed to be refined to ensure he could handle the responsibility of his calling. Eventually, God exalted Joseph to become a ruler of Egypt, only second to the King (Genesis 41:38-57). I encourage you to honor your spirit of discipline, even when it is hard and frustrating, because, in time, God will promote you according to your growth, not your goals. So, stay disciplined, even when it hurts!

Patience Is a Virtue

If you haven't noticed by now, transformation is huge to God. This divine experience is purposely orchestrated to expose your behaviors and attitudes that could destroy your destiny. Unfortunately, the exposure process typically happens while undergoing adversity of some kind. That is because it is easy to *be* good when things *are* good, but what happens when things aren't good or going the way you expected? Do you respond with patience or impatience? For example, it is easy to be patient for a flight when you know what time it will depart, but how patient are you when there is delay after delay? When you have been sitting at the airport for hours, tracking weather reports with no signs of a storm, unresponsive airline agents, and no plane in sight, are you disgruntled and full of complaints, or are you unbothered and compliant?

God uses adverse experiences, like delays, to test the authenticity of your growth. He will always give you an opportunity to show Him who you *really* are when things are not going *your* way. It is no different for purpose. How do you respond when you have done everything you were supposed to do, and nothing happens? It's as if you have held up your end of the bargain while it seems like God reneged on His promise. You have remained faithful. You have prayed and read your Bible. You may have even practiced visualizations to ensure you got "it" right, but nothing has happened. Then, what is your response? Do you cry out to God, reminding Him of all you have done? Do you question where He is? Do you feel overlooked or abandoned? Are you angry? Frustrated? Sad? What do you feel when you do not see a harvest of what you have labored so diligently to grow?

You may wonder things like:

Why is it taking so long?

Should I just give up?

Why did I even waste my time?

Why is this happening to me?

What is the point?

When are You going to follow through?

Where is my promise?

All the above questions are common when you are not reaping any *immediate* rewards from your hard work, but the truth is, your frustration is a result of impatience. You think God should deliver on His promises according to *your* timeframe.

The biggest misconception of impatience is the belief that God is supposed to answer to *you*. You feel *He* owes *you* something, and when He does not come through, the little child in you rises up, and you resort to childlike ways. You engage in temper tantrums, crying, questioning, and wondering, on the verge of throwing in the towel, but friend, your attitude is not just exposing your impatience. It's exposing your sense of entitlement. God wants to see how you will handle not getting what you want *when you want it.* Your perceived delays are not because God does not honor His promises or because He is unconcerned.

No way!

Your delays are because He cares so much for you.

Your expression of impatience shows God that you have yet to mature in a way that pleases Him, nor does it represent your readiness for such a significant purpose. You don't see results just because you want them. You must grow into a person who can handle them.

Imagine a mom interacting with her child who is visibly upset because they can't have a cookie and are told, "No, not right now." The child's attitude may reflect one of two things: A trust that breeds patience and responds with "Okay, Mommy" because they know their mom will deliver eventually, or that child may cry, scream, and kick because they must wait. The demonstration of the latter reveals the child's sense of entitlement. The child believes that because they have a want, the want should be met immediately.

Consider how your behavior is reminiscent of either of those reactions. Does your heart say, "God, I trust You and *Your* timing," or does it say, "No! I want it *now!* It's mine"? I want you to understand there is nothing wrong with wanting. The problem is how you wait for what you want. Patience means waiting *quietly* with fortitude and *without* complaint.

How have you been waiting?

If you are stuck in the process, questioning why God has not delivered yet or why it is taking so long to see your hard work pay off, I encourage you to *choose* the attitude of patience. Patience demonstrates your maturity and the authenticity of your growth.

Are you *really* self-controlled?

Do you *really* trust God?

Have you *really* grown?

This is where your growth or lack thereof is revealed in the process – when you are not receiving what you expect.

There is a misconception that some people are patient, while others are not, but friend, patience is not a personality trait. It is a *choice*. Patience is a *willingness* to refrain from reacting to anything or nothing. In this case, *nothing* is what you perceive as a lack of progress. You don't see results. You don't see quantifiable growth. You no longer see the light at the end of the tunnel, but with an attitude of patience, you choose that nothing will affect you. Patience illustrates an attitude that says, "Despite the circumstance, I will remain level-headed and humble. I refuse to be reactive."

Patience has significant benefits that safeguard you from falling into your old mode of operation. That is because patience is a preservative – it protects the integrity of your growth. However, if you choose to be impatient, you jeopardize your growth, which could slow your progress. For example, if you previously struggled with operating in discipline, you would start to see a decline in your performance again because impatience sabotages growth and productivity. Being impatient will negatively affect your thinking and distort your perspective, causing you to become discouraged and frustrated with God. However, if you choose to respond to your process with patience, you will continue to be faithful, committed, and proactive. Exercising patience validates your growth and reveals true respect for the process.

Choosing patience in difficult circumstances can feel very unnatural, but that is the point of growth. Your training requires you to outgrow old behaviors to grow into new behaviors. Producing any fruit of the Spirit is unnatural because it goes against your nature. Your nature is to be reactive, defensive, entitled, prideful, and impatient. However, those are the very traits God wants to cut away. Those attitudes destroy your character and make you ineffective for purpose, and that is why adversity is essential for growth – because it reveals the parts of you that need to be pruned. If everything is going as well as you expected, of course, you will always demonstrate the fruit of the Spirit. It is when you undergo testing that authenticates whether you are bearing *good* fruit. Unfortunately, you cannot be pruned without experiencing discomfort. Discomfort can take shape in many forms, such as setbacks, losses, and delays, but if you choose to be patient during the process, it will act as your armor against spiritual stagnation. Remember, the point of purpose is not solely for *you* to produce but for *God* to produce good fruit within you. God is concerned about the fruit of your spirit more than the fruit of your hands.

Will it be easy?

Absolutely not!

Your nature will want you to react based on what you see or feel, but that is why it is important to continue engaging your faith and partnering with God. Patience is a divine characteristic that develops through an ongoing connection with God. You cannot produce the fruit of patience without being connected to the One who provides it. Staying connected to the Lord is your key to producing the fruit of patience on your journey. Remember, you are the vine, and He is the branches. You cannot produce fruit apart from Him.

I know you may be tired of hearing, "Just be patient! It'll happen in due time!" But friend, that is the only way God can test the integrity of your growth. His Word clearly states, *"If you let patience work in you, the end result will be good. You will be mature and complete. You will be all that God wants you to be"* (James 1:4). You see, God wants you to reach your full potential, but it will require patience. Your patience proves maturation. That is the goal for your process – to grow, lacking nothing. That is why it is important to let *nothing* affect you, so God can see that you lack *nothing*.

So, what are you supposed to do while being patient?

Focus on today.

God's Word says, *"Therefore do not worry about tomorrow, for tomorrow will worry about itself. Each day has enough trouble of its own"* (Matthew 6:34). What can you do today to continue to become a person of excellence? You continue to master your skillset, not only in the area of your goals but as a person. If you have done all you can related to the opportunities you are waiting on for your purpose, there are other opportunities for growth. There is always something you can be developing.

Are you the best mom? Wife? Employee?

What other areas are you struggling with that are unrelated to the results you want to see?

Do you need to lose weight?

Do you need to spend more time with your family and with God?

The goal is to be a complete person, not just when it comes to purpose. Use this time to continue growing and developing in all areas of your life. There is an opportunity for growth every day, so do not keep looking for tomorrow's results when you can make an effective change today. Do not use today to complain and undo all the good you have done up to this point. You demonstrate patience when you put energy into other areas of your life that are just as significant to God as your obedience to your calling.

Please note, your vision is not delayed. It is in process. He assures us the vision will come to pass, slowly but surely: *"This vision is for a future time. It describes the end, and it will be fulfilled. If it seems slow in coming, wait patiently, for it will surely take place. It will not be delayed"* (Habakkuk 2:3).

The things He planned for you will not happen right away. Look at the words God chose as He demonstrates the time it will take before your vision is fulfilled: *"slowly, surely."*

Friend, if you feel like God is slow in fulfilling His promises to you, it is because He is. You desire suddenly, while God desires slowly and steadily.

Who is in a hurry here?

It certainly isn't God.

He is concerned about your spiritual development, and that kind of growth is not an overnight feat. It takes time, *slowly but surely*. Do not lose sight of the goal because you keep looking at the calendar. Respect the process by embracing patience. Allow God to test your heart as you wait patiently without complaint. In time, He will fulfill the promises attached to your obedience. Let this scripture be of some encouragement to you: *"Dear brothers and sisters, be patient as you wait for the Lord's return. Consider the farmers who patiently wait for the rains in the fall and in the spring. They eagerly look for the valuable harvest to ripen. You, too, must be patient"* (James 5:7-8).

If you have not seen the fruit of your labor yet, it may mean your fruit is too ripe. You can be eager, but do not be impatient. What you have sown *will* result in a harvest, but at the right time, so be patient without complaint!

Remember Why

If you feel discouraged and start to see a drop in your productivity, it may be time to refocus and revisit the vision.

But how?

Start by engaging your memory to *remember why you started.*

Remembering is an opportunity to reject your current attitudes to be refueled by the memory of your commitment. Revisiting your goals when tempted to compromise is a great way to fight against sabotage. I encourage you to go back to your vision board, planners, mission statements, and other visualizations you had when you committed to this journey. Ask yourself the following questions:

What was initially intriguing?

Was it my desire for more?

Was pleasing God my motivation?

Was honoring my gifts and responsibilities important to me?

Remembering reaffirms God's promises for you. Ask yourself the following questions:

What did God promise you as a result of moving forward by faith?

Did He promise you will be academically accomplished?

Did He promise you will retire at a certain age?

Did He promise financial freedom?

Did His promises include mental and emotional stability?

When you reflect on the answers to those questions, you can put things back into alignment to accomplish your goal.

Keeping your vision in plain sight is a practical way to stay enthusiastic about your goals. This will help set your intention for the day and every day to follow. This strategy is simple yet often overlooked because of its simplicity, but the truth is, remembering why you started will help you finish. That is the goal!

Chapter Five

Know Who You Are

A Broken Identity

At the start of this book, you learned that the only way to activate the fire within is by staying connected to God. Your fire is a result of the connection. In this chapter, you will learn that although the fire starts with God, the fire ultimately ends with you. Depending on the strength of your identity, *you* determine the longevity of your fire. If you struggle with knowing who you are, you will struggle with knowing how to show up for your destiny. The enemy will use your ignorance to his advantage because he knows you will be confused about your calling because you are confused about your identity. You will feel lost, defeated, insecure, and aimless, never going full throttle in your purpose.

You will question the authenticity of your calling, asking questions like:

93

Am I really supposed to be pursuing this goal?

Did God really call me?

Did I get it right?

Why me?

Those questions are symptoms of a broken identity. Any time you waddle in self-doubt and unbelief is because you do not understand that purpose has nothing to do with being capable and everything to do with being *called*. However, it is important to know *who* you are, so you will not allow the world to tell you who you are supposed to be. Society operates in a broken identity of self. The world will try to convince you that you must look a certain way, act a certain way, and have certain characteristics to achieve success. When you are bombarded with thoughts of "I am not enough. I am inadequate. I am unqualified," those are indicators you have measured your self-worth according to the world's standard. However, God is emphatic about extinguishing those lies, so you will not conform to man's way of functioning in purpose. He wants your self-view to be transformed, less focused on *what* you have and more focused on *who* you are in Him. The distinctive difference between the two is that the world's way is based on pressure, and God's way is based on faith. I believe God intentionally withholds the attributes we think are necessary for our purpose, so we can trust in Him more than we trust ourselves.

Knowing who you are requires an unwavering faith that says, "Regardless of what I appear to lack, I have been chosen, so that means I can do it." That kind of confidence sets you on fire *and* sets you apart. You will not be held back by the characteristics you do not have because you know whatever you lack means God did not need.

Whew!

Read that again.

That should bring great relief.

You have been equipped with what *He* deemed necessary to live out your calling, not what society says is necessary. Purpose is a divine assignment that does not rely on your skillset. Instead, it relies on the supernatural power of God. When you understand this, your identity can be secure because it will be rooted in the characteristics of God instead of your limitations. Your faith in Him will act as your fuel to move forward in purpose, not self-sufficiencies.

A Secure Identity

In Chapter Two, do you recall learning that the quality of your thinking will directly affect the quality of your work? In this case, the quality of self-perception will directly affect the quality of your *effort*. When you view yourself with a distorted lens, it will leave you doing little to nothing at all. But when your self-view is clear and objective, your work ethic will be positively impacted.

To be clear, identity is not an attachment to your finances, relationship status, career, or accomplishments. Those are only experiences. They are extensions of who you are and what you do. Identity has much more significance that is not defined by your performance, accomplishments, or opportunities. You are not defined by a position in the world. You are defined by your position in Christ. Identity can be best explained as *knowing you are a child of God, with a personality designed by God, with talents gifted by God for the purposes of bringing Him glory.*

Friend, your identity is who you are *to* God!

I encourage you to reread that definition until it is memorized. It will act as an anchor for you as you move forward in your purpose, and it will be a powerful tool to use when bombarded with self-limiting beliefs.

Knowing who you are offers a sense of freedom that allows you to walk confidently in your purpose without being held back by your shortcomings. This confidence allows you to operate boldly in the *authority* God has given you. The enemy, however, knows that if you define your identity apart from God, your confidence will falter between *"I can do this!"* to *"What was I thinking? I can't do this!"* There will always be inconsistencies in your performance when your identity rests in your abilities. However, when you know who you are in God, your confidence will be consistent with who He is because He never changes.

Confidence isn't *"I can do anything!"*

Confidence is *"I can do everything through Christ who gives me strength."*

Do you notice the difference?

Your power is not in your ability. Your power is found in Christ.

If you are feeling powerless on your journey, then you may have an identity crisis. If you have been plagued with thoughts of unworthiness, inadequacy, and self-doubt, then it is time to take your eyes off yourself and put them back on God.

Do you remember the story of Peter walking on water? While looking at Jesus, he successfully walked on water, but as soon as he took his eyes off Jesus, he began to sink (Matthew 14). Peter sank because he was distracted by the storm's turbulence, the winds, and the waves, and it terrified him. The same happens to you! When you take your eyes off the Lord, you start to notice everything wrong with yourself. *That is why your eyes should never be on you!* When your eyes are always on you, it is only a matter of time before you start to sink and drown in your limitations. God has chosen you, not because you are without deficiencies, but because His power is made perfect in them. Keep your eyes on Him because that will keep you securely walking in your calling.

Self-Awareness

When defining your identity, it is wise not to quantify your attributes as a sum of who you are. However, it is wise to take notice of your attributes, good and bad, for the sake of self-awareness. God's Word warns us not to think of ourselves more highly than we should because that is an identity rooted in pride. However, we are told to be sober in our self-evaluation because that is an identity rooted in humility. Operating in this level of humility understands the importance of self-awareness. God wants you to be self-aware, just not self-focused.

Simply put, self-awareness keeps you honest about yourself. When you know who you are, you can openly admit your limitations, weaknesses, and behaviors without allowing those shortcomings to define you. But a person who struggles in their identity will have a hard time looking in the mirror and admitting their limitations without destroying their self-esteem. Ironically, when you have a strong sense of who you are, it is quite the opposite. A person with a secure identity can confidently admit the following:

I know I struggle with...

I am triggered by...

I can improve in the area of…

I can do better with…

I can't do…

Those "I" statements are incredibly powerful because they do not deny uncomfortable truths. They embrace them. Acknowledging those truths breeds freedom. You are confidently admitting your limitations without being limited by them. It is understanding your potential is not contingent on your faults but solely on the fact that you have been called. However, those statements can have an adverse effect on a person who does not have a secure identity. They will feel defeated and withdraw from their purpose because they will be distracted by what they cannot seem to do instead of what they are supposed to do.

Take a moment to reflect on those statements. Do you feel empowered or discouraged? Acknowledging your attitudes and behavior in this way is the perfect opportunity to be honest with yourself without allowing your responses to destroy your confidence. Depending on your reaction, it will expose if your identity is secure in the Lord.

As you have learned, identity is who you are *to* God, while self-awareness keeps you accountable to that identity. Self-awareness does not distract you from being aware of God's authority in your life. It disputes the attitudes and behaviors that could undermine your authority. An outlook as such allows you to humbly identify areas where you can build on your strengths and improve your weaknesses. For example:

Do you lose momentum because you are easily distracted?

Do you get stuck on tasks because you have yet to master that skill?

Do you feel anxious when your deadline is approaching?

Questions like those allow you to be honest about who you are to correct the behaviors that do not align with your desired identity and goal. Without this kind of discipline, you will notice inconsistencies in your productivity because you lack accountability. When you hold yourself accountable to a higher standard, it forces you to improve to function better for your purpose. Then and only then will your behavior align with your identity and goals.

You Are What You Do

It is easy to notice other people's success because of what they have accomplished, but rarely do we consider what they have done in private to attain those goals. We rarely evaluate our behavior to achieve the level of success we admire in others. Committing to a goal is only half the battle. The battle is won if there is a commitment to the *person* who can achieve that goal. Your behavior will always be consistent with your beliefs. If you want steady progress, you must be committed to the person who responds proactively. You must have a clear understanding of the identity and habits of the successful person you want to become to achieve optimal performance and productivity.

Consider these questions when understanding the actions of another person:

Does this person wake up at 5:30 am?

Does this person commit a few minutes each day to personal development?

Does this person consistently make sacrifices?

Does this person establish routines?

Are they optimistic?

Do they set goals and persevere through excuses and adversity?

Imagine how this person looks, behaves, responds, and interacts with other people and how they talk to themselves. Then, connect with that version of who you want to be.

Once you connect with the greater version of yourself, you will start responding like that person. Productivity starts with how you identify yourself. If you try to show up with the mindset of "I can't do this. This is too hard," full of excuses and complaints, you will produce based on that negative mentality, never seeing much progress. But if you choose to show up with the mindset of "I can do all things through Christ. I am focused, committed, dedicated, and capable," you will become the trailblazer you've set out to be. Your behavior will compliment your goals or contradict them. This is why establishing a strong identity is critical because everything you do flows from how you see yourself. If you want to be clear on your purpose, consistent in your purpose, and connected to your purpose, you must commit to the behaviors that are consistent with the person you know you are called to be.

You Are...

Your struggle with identity should not come as a surprise. Satan attacks your identity because it is an attack on God. If he can get you to question your authority, it is as if you are questioning the One who created you. Satan loves nothing more than causing confusion and conflict in your relationship with the Lord. If you operate in a self-defeating mindset, it empowers the enemy to make you your own antagonist by blurring the lines of who you *think* you are and who you *really* are. But when you walk in your authority and know who you are, you are a threat to Satan. He is threatened because he cannot influence you when you are under the influence of Christ.

You see, the devil is not necessarily concerned with fighting what you are *doing*. He is threatened by who you are to God and who you are *becoming*. If your work does not transform you, you are not a threat to Satan. Jesus accomplished much in his first 30 years of life, but it wasn't until *after* He was baptized when God said, *"This is my Son, whom I love; with him, I am well pleased,"* declaring who Jesus was *to* Him that the enemy felt threatened (Matthew 3:17). The devil detests your position as a child of God, so he attacks your identity to make you compromise the effectiveness of your calling.

Take Jesus, for example. Immediately after God professed His love for Him, He was sent into the wilderness to be tempted. While in the wilderness, scripture reveals Jesus fasted for 40 days and 40 nights (Matthew 4:2). Upon completing the fast, the enemy then challenged Jesus multiple times by saying, *"If you are..."* The enemy was more concerned with *who* He was, not *what* He was doing. Satan knew Jesus was the Son of God, but he was testing Jesus' *authority* as God's Son. This is Satan's ultimate ploy – to cause you to doubt your authority as a child of God. He wants to gain victory over your destiny by causing you to second-guess who you are. If you second-guess, you are more likely to compromise or give up because your identity is not secure. But here is some good news – the same authority God has given Jesus is the same authority that lives inside you! You are powerful, but the enemy will always try to confuse your position by questioning the following:

If you are, then why don't you *do* this?

If you are, then why don't you *have* this?

If you are, *why can't* you do this?

He will question your identity to make you unsure of your authority.

If you are struggling with knowing who you are, here are several quick reminders:

You are a child of God (1 John 3:1-2).

You are chosen (1 Peter 2:9).

You are a royal priesthood (1 Peter 2:9).

You are God's special possession (1 Peter 2:9).

You are set apart (Jeremiah 1:5).

You are accepted (Romans 15:7).

You are more than a conqueror (Romans 8:37).

You are a masterpiece (Ephesians 2:10).

The truth is, *you are because He is.*

It is impossible to know who you are without knowing the character of God. How do you view the Lord? Do you see Him as an invisible deity who controls the world at a distance, or do you see Him as your good, compassionate Father who cares for you and loves you unconditionally? Your view of God will directly impact your view of yourself. If you see God as unfair and unmoved by your circumstances, you will see yourself as mistreated and unloved. If you see God as faithful, you will see yourself as an overcomer. If you see God as a forgiving God, you will see yourself as forgiven, whole, and free. What you believe about God will instinctively impact what you believe about yourself. You cannot have an identity separate from God because you are made in His image: *"So God created mankind in his own image, in the image of God he created them; male and female he created them"* (Genesis 1:27).

My eight-year-old son, Tyler, is starting to fall in love with the game of basketball; however, at times, he feels insecure and lacks confidence in his abilities. My husband took notice of this, being a former professional basketball player, and he lovingly said to Tyler, "Don't you know I was a great basketball player, so that means you are, too!" That gave Tyler a burst of confidence because he believed since he is his daddy's son, that he has what it takes, too.

Truthfully, we don't know if Tyler's athleticism will ever match his father's, and I believe it will, but at that moment, Tyler remembered who he was in relation to his father, and that changed his attitude and focus. You should take on that same attitude when you start to feel insecure or self-doubting – you have the DNA of Christ running through your blood. You are powerful and victorious! Walk in the authority of being a child of God. It pleases the Lord when you have faith, not just in who He is but who you are to Him, and never forget – *you are because He is.*

Assumed vs. Given

When I hear the phrase, "You are a product of your environment," I squirm because though that comment has been widely accepted as the truth, I disagree with that statement wholeheartedly. I understand the sentiment in theory, but realistically, it simply is not true. I believe God uses our environment to develop us, but He does not use our environment to define us. Being a single mother does not define you. Being in

103

foster care does not define you. Growing up poor does not define you. Whatever your background or circumstances, they cannot define who you are and what you can do. You must be careful not to take on an assumed identity based on a sum of your experiences because it will negatively interfere with how you view yourself. To have a healthy self-view, you must accept your God-given identity despite your experiences and environment. Genealogy and geography are man's way of determining one's potential, but when you are called by God, the authority He has given you supersedes those assumptions.

Gideon is an excellent example to understand this concept better. Gideon's story takes place during the oppression of the Israelites from the Midianite people because of their disobedience toward the Lord (Judges 6). While Gideon was hiding in a winepress from the Midianites, an angel of the Lord came to Gideon to deliver a message of deliverance for him and his people. Before the angel details God's plan to use Gideon, he addresses Gideon as a *"mighty hero"* (Judges 6:12). As the dialogue continues, Gideon refuses to take on the identity God has given him, "mighty hero," and rebuttals with excuses as to why he could not take on the charge to deliver his people out of the hands of the Midianites. Gideon says, *"How can I rescue Israel? My clan is the weakest in the whole tribe of Mannesah, and I am the least in my entire family!"* (Judges 6:11-15). Gideon was essentially saying, "I am not good enough. Look where I come from! Have you seen my family? They are insignificant! And not to mention, I am the most insignificant in my family." Gideon was confident in his responses because he was responding from his assumed identity. Gideon was so concerned with his environment that he believed he was the wrong choice for the assignment.

Many believe Gideon spoke from a place of fear, but I believe he spoke from a broken identity. Gideon fought against his God-given identity because he was so attached to his assumed identity. How attached are you to your assumed identity? Have you resisted doing the things God has called you to do because you don't see yourself the way God sees you? Do you feel insignificant?

Sometimes, we become torn between our assumed identity and our God-given identity. You may have allowed the trauma from your childhood to dictate who you are. Perhaps you were adopted, abandoned, or abused, and those experiences have warped your self-perception, subsequently making you feel unworthy, unqualified, or insignificant. I want you to understand those things do not define who you are to God. Experiences are only extensions of who you are, but they do not determine your identity. If you are operating out of brokenness and unworthiness, you must know you are operating out of your *assumed identity*. You assume because you have encountered misfortune that you are too broken to be chosen.

That is a lie!

God uses all kinds of people.

I would like to think the ones who experienced an imperfect life are typically His first choice. His Word says He likes to use the foolish to dumbfound the wise (1 Corinthians 1:27). Even if you have made some foolish mistakes or were the victim of the mistakes of others, none of that can blemish God's view of you. He called you because He wanted *you*.

People may see you from a broken perspective, but that does not mean you have to attach your identity to what they think. Do not assume you must have the perfect family or story to do a great thing for God. If you

105

feel a nudging in your spirit to pursue greatness, that should be enough. God stamped His approval over your life. If you hold on to the misguided assumptions of yourself, you will never get ahold of faith. Decide, today, you will no longer walk in the assumed identity man tries to give you but proudly receive the identity God has given you.

Gideon thought he knew who he was, but God revealed his true identity to him. God will also reveal your true identity according to how He created you. Knowing your God-given identity will then help you to step into God's plan for your life. God had planned for Gideon to be the deliverer of Israel, but he first had to change Gideon's knowledge of who he really was. Understanding your real identity enables you to rise up and accomplish mighty things Knowing who you are helps you realize what you can do.

Called > Qualified

The biggest misconception about pursuing greatness is that you must be qualified. People strive to get more education, training, and credibility, but when you are truly called, God will leverage what you already have. This is not to say education or training is not important. They just are not the focus. But people who struggle with an identity crisis are constantly striving to make themselves feel qualified versus knowing they already are qualified.

Moses is one of the greatest examples of one being subjected to this kind of identity crisis. You see, when God told Moses he was called to lead the Israelite slaves into freedom, Moses immediately focused on his insecurities. Moses started ticking off a list of things he was not good at because he did not feel like he was qualified for such a huge purpose. Moses basically said, "How am I to lead when I can barely speak? I stutter. I am not articulate. Why me?" However, God did not reconsider His choice. Do you think God was stumped and thought, "Aw, man! I chose the wrong guy. He can't speak well, let alone lead"? Absolutely not! In fact, God did not entertain Moses' insecurities. Instead, God demonstrated His power to redirect Moses' focus to the Lord.

God did this by encouraging Moses to look at what he *did* have. God responded to Moses' excuses by asking him, "What's that in your hand?" God was essentially saying, "Stop telling Me what you don't have and what you cannot do. I didn't ask you that. Tell Me what you *do* have – what is in your hand?" Then, God takes what Moses has, a stick, and fills it with His power. The stick transformed into a snake and back to a stick because of God's power. God was showing Moses that he did not have to have anything significant to be called. He just needed to acknowledge the little he did have for God to use. God wants to leverage what you *do* have.

As Moses obediently responded to the calling over his life, he took his stick, the only thing he had, and successfully led the slaves out of Egypt. God took Moses' *little* and infused His great power into it. Friend, God wants to do the same for you. God can use anything you are willing to offer Him. If He can use a stick, surely, He can use you and whatever you *do* have!

If you have the gift of writing, but insecurities make you put down your pen, pick it up!

If you have the gift to sing but are untrained, use your voice and pick it up!

If you want to teach a Bible study but have never taught a class, pick up your Bible!

God is saying to pick up whatever you keep trying to put down. The power is there, but you must allow God to access it. Allow God to activate His power in what you *do* have because that is what He wants to use. You do not need what appears to be missing. You need what already exists. Who you are and what you have is enough for God. Do not be held back because of your weaknesses. Instead, boast in them because His power infuses your weaknesses to become your strength (2 Corinthians 12: 9-10).

Live in Truth

To apply these principles to your life, you must understand the importance of living in truth. *Living in truth* protects your self-esteem and prevents you from falling victim to self-defeat.

Have you ever heard the phrase, "Don't bring a knife to a gunfight"? This figure of speech means the person with a knife is at a disadvantage because a knife does not adequately equip one to fight against their opponent. The same notion applies when it comes to fighting against Satan when he attacks your identity. You will surely be outmatched if you are not properly equipped for the nature of this battle. When confronted with temptations to define your identity separate from God, you must know how to respond to the enemy. You cannot rely on social media quotes or affirmations to act as a line of defense against the enemy. You must use the Word of God and declare *His* truth. If you don't, Satan will destroy your confidence and self-esteem because anything you declare apart from God's Word will be like quicksand to your confidence.

There is no security in anything other than *living in truth* to God's Word. When you live in truth to God's Word, Satan is no match for you. He will always be defeated when you are armed with biblical ammunition.

As previously stated, your confidence is not connected to your appearance, bloodline, or gifts. Confidence built on self will surely fizzle. God's Word is the foundation of your confidence, and if you do not live in truth to His Word, you will consistently struggle with the lies of Satan. He will tell you things like:

You aren't good enough.

You aren't smart enough.

You aren't attractive enough.

You aren't talented enough.

You aren't cut out for the job.

Unfortunately, you will start to believe him if you do not live in truth to who God is and what He says about you. When you live in truth, you can identify Satan's lies and overcome them.

Jesus is the perfect example of one who lived in truth, and the interaction between Him and Satan is evident of this. Earlier, I referenced Matthew 4, when Satan tempted Jesus on multiple occasions by saying, *"If you are...,"* challenging Jesus' authority as God's Son. However, Jesus knew scripture and used it as His defense, which made Satan's tactics ineffective. Jesus successfully withstood Satan's temptations because He was armed with God's Word and *trusted* that power. *Trusting* the truth of God's Word is where your authority comes from.

If you read Matthew 4, you will notice how the enemy also used scripture while challenging Jesus' identity. However, Satan will always use the truth deceptively. Sometimes, the enemy will use the truth against you, the truth you know about yourself or your circumstances, to deceive you from walking in the authority God has given you. His truths can sound like the following:

You are overweight.

You have a speech impediment.

You don't have a degree.

You don't have any money in the bank.

You have bad credit.

All those statements are aimed to destroy your confidence and self-esteem.

The enemy will use real insecurities, flaws, past mistakes, and hidden shame for the sole purpose of tearing you down. Beware of the so-called "truths" Satan brings to you. Though the accusations may be factual, that does not mean those are *reliable* truths about who you are in Christ. Satan attacks your identity because he knows if he can destroy your confidence in the natural, he can disrupt your divine purpose. Satan's goal is for you to live beneath your potential because he knows there is no power there.

However, when you know God's truth, you can respond like Jesus, as He was not swayed by the enemy's manipulation of God's Word. Jesus lived in truth to God's Word and responded confidently: *"The scriptures also say, 'You must not test the Lord your God'"* (Matthew 4:7). In the face of the enemy, you must be ready to respond with, "The scriptures also say…" Being knowledgeable of these truths only comes from spending time in God's Word. So, you must read it! Spend time learning scripture because it is your defense against Satan.

What does the enemy use against you to destroy your confidence?

Past mistakes?

Flaws?

Current circumstances?

No matter what the enemy uses against you, the Bible has what you need to defend yourself with *comforting truths* to disarm the enemy's attacks. The same happened to Jesus when He fought back with God's Word – the devil went away. The devil left Jesus alone because Jesus activated His authority when He trusted in the Word of God.

Jesus lived in truth!

The devil brought a knife to a gunfight and lost!

Satan will always be at a disadvantage when you are armed with the truth of God's Word. You must know how to beat the enemy at his own game. When you live in truth, he will flee from you, too! This is the only way to securely operate in your God-given identity so that you can accomplish the great things He has predestined for you.

Nothing to Prove

What was so brilliant about Jesus' encounter with Satan was His ability to prove who He was without having to prove it by demonstration. When the enemy told Jesus, *"If you are the Son of God, tell these stones to become loaves of bread"* (Matthew 4:3). Jesus replied, *"No! The Scriptures say, 'People do not live by bread alone but by every word that comes from the mouth of God'"* (Matthew 4:4). Jesus did not react to Satan from a place of ego. Instead, He responded from a place of *reverence*. He pointed the enemy's attention back to His Heavenly Father. Jesus did not rely on His power to prove His authority. Instead, He acknowledged God's authority. Jesus knew He did not have to prove who He was because He was proof of God.

When you do what God has instructed you to do for His purposes, your *life* is proof of God's authority and His power working in you. You already measure up because God did the pouring! Do not ever feel like you must display your strengths, accomplishments, gifts, and abilities for the sake of man. You lose credibility with God when trying to prove yourself to the world. Paul poses this rhetorical question in Galatians 1:10: *"Am I now trying to win the approval of human beings or of God? Or am I trying to please people? If I were still trying to please people, I would not be a servant of Christ."*

Proving yourself to people is self-serving, not a reflection of serving the Lord.

You are not gifted for the purposes of recognition or public opinion, but Satan will present many ways for you to steal God's glory for yourself. The enemy will prompt you to post on social media to show off or prove you are accomplishing your goals. Your sharing may seem harmless, but your ego will have you saying, "Look! I did *this*. I'm doing *that*. Look at what I *will* do." He will entice you to prematurely share upcoming projects or boast about what you are currently doing to distract you from exalting God to exalting yourself. Friend, you must remember you are gifted because you are chosen to do a special work *for* God, not for self-importance. I plead with you not to fall down that slippery slope of ego. The ego will drag you away from being a representation of God to acting as a god. Ego desires praise and glory, and the more you receive, the more you want, creating a sin that not only robs you of your full destiny but your position with the Lord. You can't get friendly with pride and think God is pleased with you or your efforts. The Bible says those selfish desires make you an adulterer to God (James 4:4). Remaining humble is your way of staying faithful to Him. Whenever you feel tempted to prove yourself, redirect your energy to glorifying the Lord, as this will keep you humbly positioned under God, not above Him.

While operating in your purpose, you must have the mindset of "My gift is proof that I am chosen. I don't have to prove I am chosen. I only have to work hard *because* I have been chosen." A person who fully understands the gift of being chosen recognizes flaunting their gift does not solidify their identity. Flaunting destroys it. A secure identity does not seek to be seen or needs to boast. A person who is unsure of their power will try to convince others of their ability because they are unsure of it themselves. Proving is rooted in insecurity and uncertainty. When you know who you are, you will not be distracted by showing and telling because it will be revealed on its own in God's appointed time.

When you understand this concept of having nothing to prove, you will also understand the importance of moving when God tells you, not when triggered by the enemy. The enemy will often try to rush you to move out of step with God to showcase your gifts to rob God of His glory. The same tactic was used on Jesus. When He refused to demonstrate His power when tempted by the enemy, it was because He understood God's timing was more important than His ego. Jesus did not rush because He didn't need to. He knew He was to demonstrate His power at an appointed time. Friend, you must exercise the same restraint when tempted to rush a process that God has yet to release you to show. When Jesus finally demonstrated His authority by turning water into wine, it was necessary and when God got the most glory. When you share prematurely, you are not fulfilling a significant need. You are only feeding the need of your ego. Your gifting should only fully manifest when God says it is time and when it is needed. When Jesus multiplied the fish and bread, it was because it was necessary. Please know, when it is time for God to reveal your gifting, it will be when it is necessary and to bring Him the glory.

Philippians 2:6-7 shares the mindset Jesus had when it came to being grounded in a secure identity without desiring God's glory: "*Who, being in very nature God, did not consider equality with God something to be used to his own advantage; rather he made himself nothing by taking the very nature of a servant.*"

Jesus understood the principle of position – acting out of service and not self-interest. He could have proved He was the Messiah by flaunting His power in the face of the enemy or His persecutors, but He defeated His ego by bringing honor back to God. That is how you overcome the need to prove yourself – taking your eyes off yourself and directing your eyes back to God. Always remember – you have nothing to prove because you have already been approved by the One who matters – your Heavenly Father.

Comparison

There are two forms of comparison you need to keep on your radar. Most people assume comparison is a negative use of energy that destroys contentment and confidence, which I wholeheartedly agree with. However, comparison, when used properly, can be surprisingly beneficial, too. Comparison is a unique response that uncovers a secure or broken identity. Your use of comparison reveals whether you have a healthy self-view. This subchapter will contrast how an unhealthy use of comparison can destroy your identity to how a healthy use of comparison can positively affect your life.

Comparison is said to be a thief of joy, but comparison is a thief of identity when used in an unhealthy state. It is a subtle yet rebellious mindset to keep you inactive and confused about who you are and what you can achieve. Ironically, comparison is a form of self-awareness that can negatively or positively impact the relationship you have with yourself.

Comparison *seems* to be more focused on another individual, what they have, and their abilities. However, comparison reveals more about *you* than about another person. Your extreme focus on your insecurities automatically draws your attention to those who do not *appear* to have the same hang-ups. However, they are not the focus. The real focus is what you believe is wrong with yourself or what you believe you lack. Your divided attention comes from your discontentment, subsequently leaving you discouraged and unproductive.

As mentioned earlier, destiny cannot thrive or survive on a broken identity. If you have been stuck in the comparison game that has negatively affected you, it is most likely you are stuck in the pursuit of your purpose, too, but the good news is that you can break free from this trap by simply changing your belief. In this unhealthy state, the need to compare is rooted in a belief that something is missing in your life, whether characteristically, financially, or your abilities. All in all, it makes you *believe* you are not enough.

The problem with this form of comparison is that it collects data out of context. The information is out of context because comparison can only quantify what it sees (perception), not what it knows (knowledge). Comparison is a biased assessment measured by your insecurities to those who appear to have more of what you believe you lack. The game of comparison is not based on wisdom. It is based on assumptions. You assume you are inferior or superior based on a distorted belief about yourself. However, unhealthy comparison fails to acknowledge what is *truly* lacking. Your struggle with comparison is not because of your lack of finances, abilities, or characteristics. You need to compare is due to your lack of faith. Your *unbelief* creates fantasies of who you *could* be if only you had more – more money, more experience, more resources, and more personality... *more.* Your perceived lack is because of your distorted mentality, not a distorted reality. You do not need more of anything to be happy or to accomplish your goals. You only need more faith!

You must believe you are enough.

You must believe you have enough.

God did not make a mistake with how He created you. You must stop thinking God scaled back when it came to you. God knows what you need, and it rarely comes in the form you expect. Your scarcity mindset is destroying what you need more of… faith!

Friend, faith is not only believing in God. Faith also believes what God says about you. He said you are a masterpiece. You are set apart! God created you just the way He saw fit, lacking nothing. If you negatively compare yourself to another person, you will only notice what you do not have, not what you truly need. All you need is more faith. You do not need more of what "they" have but more of what matters to God – faith. He only asks that you believe, not in yourself, but Him. Stop comparing, so you can start conquering your dreams. You cannot be victorious with a defeated mindset.

When comparison is misappropriated, it will create an attitude of helplessness, hopelessness, and hatefulness. On the contrary, positive comparison can inspire great hope. For those who properly apply comparison, it can be a source of motivation. If you have a mindset based on scarcity, you will be trapped between feeling helpless and hateful. Feeling helpless will make you think things like, "I can't do that" and "I don't have the resources." Those thoughts result in feeling discouraged and unproductive.

Another misuse of comparison is to hate on someone else. Hating someone is for the purpose of tearing them down, no matter how great they are. This is a means to affirm yourself because magnifying their flaws seem to make your flaws smaller. In some strange way, identifying their areas of weakness makes you feel a sense of security. However, that is not true security because it is based on a biased assessment of hate, not acceptance. You will start to say things like, "Who does she think she is?!" and "She's so overrated!" Those thoughts encourage you to pick other people apart so that you can feel better about yourself. That kind of mindset starts to give birth to jealousy and self-defeat. Neither of those forms of comparison encourage productivity. Instead, those forms of comparison project negativity and insecurity.

On the flip side, when comparison is used appropriately, it inspires hope! If you notice someone you respect, you can use their success to

117

compare your discipline to theirs, not your talent. Hope will cause you to be more curious than critical. You will say things like, "Wow! How did she get there? She is so inspiring. I admire her" and "If she can do it, I can do it, too!" You are not picking her apart. Instead, you are observing her greatness to motivate you to tap more into *your* greatness. You are not concerned with being like her or being better than her. You are focused on being a better version of *yourself.* This kind of comparison will motivate you to *do* more, not that you need to *be* more. This mindset will not destroy your confidence. It will actually add to it.

The positive effect of a healthy form of comparison improves your performance and productivity. Isn't that the ultimate goal, to improve? You will be motivated to do more of what you were called to do, which will naturally produce more confidence. Your desire to show up and perform will distract you from your need to negatively compare yourself to others. You will be so busy producing that you will not have time to reduce who you are to someone else.

You must decide if you will allow comparison to stop you or be the fuel to keep you going. Will you use comparison to your benefit or your detriment? The unhealthy state of comparison will keep you feeling defeated and unworthy, but comparison in a healthy way could be used as fuel to add to your fire. Will you choose to allow comparison to undermine your self-worth and destroy your confidence, or will you allow a good use of comparison to act as motivation to become a better version of you? The choice is up to you.

Final Thoughts

If you are reading this, I am proud of you. I am proud that you are persisting in becoming the person God created you to be. You did not just "read another book." You explored a new way to grow, honor your calling, and learn new techniques to disarm the enemy's attacks. While seeking significant change, you are doing whatever it takes, by any means necessary. You are refusing to allow your excuses to become a refuge to escape your calling. You are refusing to allow your fear, insecurities, and a distorted perspective to destroy your destiny and the purpose that lives within you. You chose the difficult road of perseverance, and friend, you must continue to choose this path. Perseverance is not an easy feat, as you know. It is a transformative characteristic that produces the character, grit, and effectiveness that only comes through effort, faith, and discouragement.

Yet, you are winning.

It is not about the tangible things you gain. It is about the growth you experience. It is about renewing your mind to know God's perfect Will for your life. It is about trusting in God, not in your gift. It is about uncovering your deepest fears and crushing them by faith. All in all, you not only endure, but you also thrive. That is the result of perseverance.

You are better.

You are stronger.

You are resolute.

You are a finisher.

You will come face-to-face with your weaknesses, but they ultimately become steppingstones for greatness. Your admission to those shortcomings grants God full access to infuse His supernatural power within you. So, as you move forward, do not close this book as if this is the end of your journey. This is only the beginning, the beginning of extinguishing the lies that have previously prevented you from walking in your authority. It is the beginning of a deeper connection with you and the Lord. It is the beginning of overcoming self-defeating habits. It is the beginning of a better you who gets the job done.

Passively reading this book will not improve your life, just as wearing new workout clothes without exercising will not get you into shape. You must apply the information consistently. Transformation only occurs if you apply it. As powerful and transformative as God's Word is, it explicitly states: "*But do not just listen to God's word. You must do what it says,*" and goes on to say, '*If you do what it says and don't forget what you heard, then God will bless you for doing it*'" (James 1: 22, 25).

You will be blessed if you do what you know you should do. Your destiny hinges on your obedience. This goes beyond motivation, confidence, and skillset. This is about following through with what God called you to do despite your emotions. Get familiar with this book.

Highlight passages.

Take notes.

Journal your discoveries.

Study it.

But don't study my words. Study the scriptures that accompany the insight shared within the pages. Learn His Word and apply the practical strategies shared in the book to help you throughout your journey of purpose.

When you start to feel burned out or depleted, you will be quickly reminded in "Stay Connected" of your need to spend quality time with God to regain your momentum and motivation. When you start to lose sight of the goal and find yourself complaining about your workload, "Perspective is Key" will pull you out of your pity party and remind you of your calling's privilege and responsibility by changing the way you think.

Chapter Three, Address Your Fears, is your go-to chapter whenever you sense your momentum slowing down due to your fear of failure, outside opinions, and so forth. This chapter will remind you of the necessity of your fear and equip you with the courage you need to keep moving forward.

Reread "Respect the Process" when you are frustrated, discouraged, and on the verge of giving up because the journey may seem painfully difficult and never-ending. This chapter will encourage your faith and help you develop the strength and character that position you for success.

"Knowing Who You Are" will remind you that you were chosen by God, so you do not need to rely on your abilities. When you feel your identity is constantly overcome with thoughts of being unqualified or not good enough, this chapter will remind you of where real confidence comes from.

I wrote this book because, honestly, I needed it. But now, I understand so many of His people need it, too. This is your blueprint as much as it is mine. Although I wrote it, I still need it and refer to it every time I experience any of the symptoms that interrupt my progress. And friend, you, too, will come face-to-face with reoccurring struggles that will try to stop your progress. Whenever you start to experience any of your past destructive patterns, quickly grab your Bible and this book to remember the strategies God revealed to you.

The real work starts now.

With love,

ERICKA

About the Author: Ericka Ellis

Ericka Ellis, once an abused foster child and college dropout, chose to become a victor instead of a victim. She graduated magna cum laude from Purdue University with a master's degree in strategic management and a bachelor's degree in organizational leadership. Ericka went on to become a published author, award-winning philanthropist, and speaker, and life performance strategist known as "The Fire Starter," who ignites her peers into action. As a Fire Starter, Ericka breaks the mental barriers that interfere with one's performance and productivity through her SPARK method, which results in positive can-do attitudes, higher levels of productivity, greater performance, and happiness.

Ericka and her husband, Ty Ellis, share a passion for spiritual and personal development. Thus, Ericka co-founded The Ellis Performance Group, a performance consulting company that specializes in *people*. The Ellis Performance Group ventures include workshops, seminars, conferences, podcasts, books, retreats, and corporate training. As an advocate for foster youth, Ericka founded the non-profit (501c3), Think.Love. Smart, with a mission to "move foster girls forward."

Ericka has been featured on ABC, CBS, *D Magazine*, and *Dallas Weekly*, to name a few. Ericka has been recognized as "Texan With Character" by CBS and named "Person of Excellence of the Year" and "Top Eight Influencers of Dallas" for her work in the community.

To learn more about Ericka's keynotes, leadership coaching, and workshops or to book Ericka for your event, visit www.erickaellis.com. Ericka looks forward to customizing a tailored program for your next event!

Stay Connected to Ericka

Visit the website www.erickaellis.com

Receive the newsletter.

Attend a workshop.

Follow Ericka on Twitter @erickaellis

Like Ericka on Facebook @iamerickaellis

Follow Ericka on Instagram @erickaellis

For more information, visit www.erickaellis.com

Made in the USA
Columbia, SC
15 May 2021